You Smile When You Show Me Grace

Michelle Thooft

Cover Design by Mark Ewert

PUBLISHED BY SWORD AND TROWEL PRESS

ISBN- 978-0-9723462-1-4

Disclaimer Statement: Much of what I have learned over the years has come from others who have shared their journeys through speaking or text. I have tried to source everything at the end of this book, even if I can't remember exactly where it was said or written but I remember *who* said it. I sincerely apologize if I missed anyone and would be happy to source you and give you credit and link to your resources on our webpage. I am so thankful for all of you who have shaped my life, and I want the world to know who you are.

The title of this book, *You Smile When You Show Me Grace*, is a line adapted from a DC Talk song, "Minds Eye." I tried to get their permission to use it, but they haven't answered my emails. ☺
DC Talk, "Mind's Eye." *Jesus Freak*. The ForeFront Communications Group, 1995. CD.

I dedicate this book to my family

Grace: You really are our shining sword. You're amazing and fun and sensitive and intuitive and thoughtful and creative and slightly crazy. You are one of my favorite people in the whole world.

Ilsa: You really are our seer. You see stuff I never see, both on paper and in songs and in people and in dreams. I think if anyone can hear animals talk, it's you. Your voice makes me cry. And you keep us all laughing. You're one of my favorite people in the whole world.

Maddie: You really are our "lover-on-purpose." You purposely love us all. I can see the effort you put into it, and I am inspired and encouraged. It makes your beauty and tenderness even more beautiful. You are one of my favorite people in the whole world.

Elijah: You are our "boy-joy." You are so much fun to have around. Your little boy insights knock us all over and prompt countless Facebook posts. You are so smart and sweet it shocks me sometimes. You are one of my favorite people in the whole world.

Phil: I remember the day I realized that I didn't want to live my life without you. I still know that. You were the best decision I ever made, and you're the best friend I have ever had. Thank you for your endless love and support and encouragement. You are my favorite person in the whole world.

Prologue

"Is there a single person on whom I can press belief?
No sir.
All I can do is say, Here's how it went. Here's what I saw.
I've been there and am going back.
Make of it what you will."

Leif Enger, *Peace Like a River*

As soon as I learned it was a "writing contest," I thought I might win.

We had been training all winter for our first triathlon. Race day was early June. The Trinona Triathlon had partnered with We-no-nah Canoe to give away a beautiful canoe, painted in the Trinona colors and logo. You had to write a blurb about why you "deserved" to win it on their Facebook page.

I don't feel I "deserved" it. I have never felt like I deserved any of this. It's just my extravagant God-Dad that keeps lavishing all this on me. It makes me want to represent Him well, with the same love, acceptance, and proud-father delight that He has shown me.

You have to understand the back story here. When I was 23 I gave a beautiful baby boy named Sam a family through adoption. On his 20th birthday I had gotten a call from his mom, Kiki, with the news that he had asked about us and wanted to meet us. You will read about that in this book. So not only did we meet him after twenty years, but he and his family were coming to Winona, the city where he was born, to cheer us on in our first triathlon, and meet the extended family.

My parents have been divorced for over thirty years, and for the first time, my mom invited my dad to a gathering, and my dad invited my mom. So, I simply told We-no-nah Canoe and the Trinona this story, in

1

about a paragraph. It was the reunion of a lifetime, a dream and hope come true for so many people. It was the reuniting of more than a mother and son; it was the reuniting of a family long estranged. It all happened at the Trinona, and I wanted them to know that their event was hosting such a beautiful thing.

The canoe would be icing on all this cake. That's what I told them.

And I won. This is a story that just keeps giving and giving, in so many ways. I hope it gives to you as well. In fact, I hope you run wild with hope.

chapter one

Frodo: "I wish the ring had never come to me. I wish none of this had ever happened."
Gandalf: "So do all who live to see such times. But that is not for them to decide. All you have to decide is what to do with the time given you."

J.R.R. Tolkien, *The Fellowship of the Ring*

My window overlooked Lake Superior. I can still see it clearly. Directly below was a line of clay pots with hopeful pansy plants; then the deep, sloping lawn stretched about a hundred yards to the beach. This picture, framed in French window glass, was dotted with just enough birch and spruce to keep the lawn green with patches of fragrant pine underneath. It was late spring, so the window was almost always open, and cool breezes off the lake were like a reviving Spirit breath. When I wasn't working in the restaurant and lodge I was living in, the Lake Superior waves and the occasional lonesome call of a single, mate-less loon were the only sounds I heard.

I had worked many summers at Naniboujou Lodge, earning money for college. This summer was different. Single and pregnant, I spent hours in front of that window: reading, writing, listening, praying, crying, thinking. Grappling with God like Jacob wrestled the angel, I dutifully followed my thoughts through the pain and suffering and separation and grieving and loss, all yet to come in my scenario. In that place, God's voice began to feel real and familiar to me. I started to understand more deeply what it meant that He loved me. Unlike the mate-less loon, I was not alone.

A month earlier, during finals week, I had received the positive test result of my suspected pregnancy. The suspicion alone was shattering as

I was a fairly active Christian on campus, a leader in various Christian fellowship groups. Worse, I had no boyfriend or fiancé. My pregnancy resulted from living a second life filled with alcohol, bar hopping and flirting, eventually ending in a one-night stand with a fellow-college student I didn't know.

One of the first things I did was go to a bookstore and try to find a book written by someone who had survived this. Not a happily-expecting-mother-and-husband book, but something written by someone who was as terrified as I was, who felt as alone as I did. Everyone said they were out there-didn't anyone write anything down? There was nothing. I left the store determined that I *would* write, and that, someday, another woman would walk into a bookstore and leave knowing she wasn't alone.

Thus my pen and notebook became my constant companions. This was my first journal entry:

May, 1989

I'm 23 years old, a college senior, unmarried, and pregnant. I know from the start who I write these words to: you, a woman like me who finds yourself pregnant and alone. Everyone will be shocked, right? Nobody, especially you, ever thought you would end up pregnant. In my case, it was my first experience with sex and not just fooling around. It was an awkward, botched attempt, but apparently enough.

I was in my final month of college when I started feeling funny, and I got into the habit of taking a nap every day. I thought it was stress. Then I was late, and I'm never late.

After a week had passed, I went to our local free clinic with a friend and had a test done. It was negative. But the doctor couldn't explain my symptoms. She told me to come back in a week if nothing had changed. I returned and tested positive.

Since I had suspected the worst, I believed I would be prepared for the worst. But when the doctor said, "Well, your test read positive this time," I can only describe my feelings as hidden and hysterical, like a volcano that hadn't erupted yet.

Looking back now, I can tell you that although I sat there on that examination table fairly calmly, hysteria did indeed take over my mind. Inside, I reacted, I cried, I panicked. Darkness overwhelmed me. The doctor was sitting on a chair with her back against the door. I remember thinking that I couldn't get out. She asked me if it was a surprise, and I answered yes. Even though I had suspected, I hadn't really believed I could be pregnant. She asked me if I had thought about what I wanted to do. I answered, "I guess I'll keep it." She asked about the father and I told her I didn't know. The fact was, I did know. I had met him at a frat party and hadn't seen him since.

"You do know that you have other options, don't you?" she said, leaning forward. I can't remember her face.

"You mean abortion?" I asked. She nodded. "Where?"

"You can have one done in St. Paul."

"What do they do?" I asked hopefully. The temptation was huge: to have this quietly taken care of, to not have to face the humiliation. But something nagged at me that there was more to it.

"Vacuum suction," she said flatly. "The procedure is short." She leaned back against her chair.

Pain. Fear. Confusion. My head swam. It was hard to breathe. How could this be happening? There was no way out without pain. There was always a way out, wasn't there? I could do two or three or four things at once. I had never hit a stone wall like this.

But in the midst of this flood of emotions, something inside told me that I couldn't abort. Physically, yes, I could, but it wouldn't solve anything. I would kill a child. Why? So I could live with the pain of knowing I had taken a life – a life that wasn't able to defend itself- for the rest of my days? So I could face the possibility of death or mutilation myself? So I could be reminded of my foolishness and my selfishness forever? I remember these hard thoughts that ran through my mind; hard thoughts for me alone. It would be selfish of me to kill this baby to cover up my own sin or to save myself humiliation or embarrassment. It would be selfish of me not to give anyone else the chance to love him. It would be selfish of me not to let him keep his life. No one would know, maybe, *but God.* He had known this baby before I had. He already knew his name, his life, his days.

No, I could not abort this child. I'm not sure how all that went through my head in those few moments, but it did.

So, I left the clinic that clear spring day sure I had made the right choice, to let my child live, but terrified of the road ahead. How could I be a mother? I who had never even *liked* children? I who had been a terrible babysitter? I who had been *defined* as selfish by those who knew me?

How could anyone, anything, fix this?

Fast forward with me twenty-three years. You have just read the original journal (in bold text) that I wrote twenty three years ago while going through the pregnancy with Sam, and the original text of *The Gift of Sam*, written and published ten years ago. The rest of this book will be the original journals from *The Gift of Sam* and most of the original text, but with my voice today. We have met Sam now, and he is part of our lives. His name is Ian, and I will call him that for the rest of this book.

I wanted to give you all of this, as I experienced it, in one book. Being pregnant with him, giving him up, living without him for twenty years, writing the original book, and now, having him part of our lives. I can stand outside of it and say "it's a beautiful story. It will help you understand your life." After all, we all face terrifying situations. Yours may not be a crisis pregnancy, but comfort speaks in any language.

Today, Ian is a natural part of our family. He attends a university two hours away, and spends weekends with us when he can. We know him now as Ian, or "E," or "man-cub" or "darling." He'll even answer to "Sam" or "Sammy-boy" sometimes. I call him all those things, and he calls me "mama."

I love my boy. I am so incredibly grateful for his life, and grateful that I gave him his. He is my beautiful boy, who is now a man, and he is planning to marry a lovely girl next summer.

I have been rewarded thousands of times over for honoring his life, even when I couldn't see it.

The only thing I have regretted over the years since *The Gift of Sam* was published the first time is that I did not share my love for women who have had abortions. I was talking about *me* when I said things like *"So I could live with the pain of knowing I had taken a life – a life that wasn't able to defend itself- for the rest of my days? So I could face the possibility of death or mutilation myself? So I could be reminded of my foolishness and my selfishness forever?"* I was not talking about anyone else when I wrote those words. I was not pointing a finger, unless it was at me.

I just want to say, if you have had an abortion and are reading this book: I am not the hero and you the villain. You and I have faced the same thing and made our decisions. I do not judge you for yours. I have hard thoughts for the industry that used you, but I keep them to myself. You will never get anything but acceptance and words of healing from me.

And so, let's keep reading the story, and I will fill you in on all the changes since I wrote it first. It truly is a story of life, hope, healing, and learning to know God and believe He loves us and isn't mad at us. It's about faith and growth in the hardest times. It's about forgiveness and leaving the past behind and growing into your destiny. Really, it's a love story between God and me, and God and you. Whatever difficulty you are facing, whatever the crisis, you are loved and you are not alone.

chapter two

"Let me say for now that we knew once the Creation was broken, true fathering would be much more lacking than mothering. Don't misunderstand me, both are needed- but an emphasis on fathering is necessary because of the enormity of its absence"

William Paul Young, *The Shack*

Still in shock, I left the health office and walked three blocks to my sister's apartment. My mind seemed to shut out all other functions to try to cope with this bomb. What would the baby's father say? What would *my* father say? My parents were divorced and remarried: I had four of them to tell. I was the last person anyone would suspect of getting into this. Everyone would be shocked, because I was always the kid who didn't get into much trouble. In addition to being a steady "B" student, I had never partied or even spent much time out except for youth group events.

As a child of divorce, the center of my little-girl world was broken. Feelings of insecurity grew throughout my childhood into my teen years. Fear was with me wherever I went. Food met a need, or so I thought, and I was chubby. At school, I avoided people as much as possible, and then escaped home to eat and sit in front of the television, like a hobbit. Everything seen was believed: in order to be loved by a man you had to be slim, beautiful, and athletic. This message was plastered all over the teen magazines I read and in the television and movies I saw and the music I heard. My parents were trying to live with their own wounds and didn't know how to help me deal with these messages; they didn't know the struggles they needed to address in me. My mom was there for us as much as a single mother could be, working full time and teaching piano after school to make ends meet: she worked hard and never complained, at least not to us. When we had needs, she stopped what she was doing and met them. She married a man who loved us like his own children and still does. My father was remarried, and although my sisters and I spent time with him and my step-mom and later with my younger brother, we didn't really *talk*. And one of my main love languages, how I hear that you love me, is "words of affirmation." I didn't hear the words, literally or figuratively, that I was beautiful or smart or fun. I don't think my parents ever heard that from any of their parents, and so it goes.

I "found Jesus" at a camp when I was 16. I knew Him, I knew He was with me all those years, but I guess I made it official at teen camp. It changed something in me. I somehow received deeper understanding of this love at camp. When I went home and told my family, my parents were respectful of my faith, but didn't share it. I was pretty zealous and excited. My mom said that she would ask me if I felt the same in ten years. She might have thought it would be something that would wear off with time.

That was thirty years ago. She has never asked, but I don't think she has had to. I have learned to be respectful of how she thinks and believes, and although we still don't share faith, we share a lot of other things. Today, my dad and I share our faith. My relationship with all of my parents just keeps getting better.

Do you know what I think Christianity is all about? Finding your way home. This is how I see it, and you don't have to agree with me. I will still think you're amazing and talented and fun.

I believe God created the world, the universe, everything. He created man and woman, Adam and Eve, and he put them in a garden. He gave them everything they needed. And he gave them something really important: freedom to manage themselves. He put everything in front of them, gave them freedom to choose, and told them what choices would have good results and what choices would have negative results.

So they walked together, talked together, played together, took care of the garden, named animals, and who knows what else. Sounds like fun. Which is seriously the understatement of the year, if you'll pardon the cliché.

But, just like all the great stories, there was an enemy, waiting to shred it all. God had created a being that in the beginning was beautiful and fun, kind of like Loki in *The Avengers*. But greed got the better of him, and he decided that he wanted to be the King. And like Loki, he was banished. This real-life enemy's name is Satan. Like Loki, he couldn't kill the King, or his son. So what does any mobster do when he can't hurt the one he wants?

He goes after their kids.

This is how it played out in real life: The things that Satan wanted-power, glory, beauty, strength —were lavished on us. Adam and Eve owned it all: they had been given the earth, to tend it and care for it. In an effort to gain the control he wanted, Satan showed up in the garden as a snake, and tricked Eve into eating from a tree that God warned them about.

Eve has gotten a bad rap for this for centuries. The thing that some people don't seem to remember is that Adam was standing right there next to her. And he bailed. He knew what was right and wrong, and he went passive on her. Rather than say, "Hey, darling, this isn't a good idea. Let's talk about this. Let's ask God about it," he took the fruit she gave him, and they both ate it.

I can only imagine how all of the earth and sky wailed at that moment. All the glory that had been lavished on God's creation: lost. Our enemy, Satan, now had power because Adam and Eve had agreed with him. Satan only gets power through agreement. And worse, "sin" had entered the world. "Sin" is an archery term, and it means "missing the mark." God is perfect, and He created us to be perfect with Him. Adam and Eve made a choice that "missed the mark" and brought utter destruction and death into the world. That choice then was free to flow into all the generations to come. And it separated us from God, the one Person who knew us and loved us completely.

Imagine the loneliness.

Everything changed. Broken was the relational perfection between men and women and God. Women now endured pain in childbirth. Death happened. Adam had to toil to make a garden work. Beauty and strength were tarnished. All of creation was shattered, losing the perfection. Sometimes I think the reason we long so much for a beautiful home with landscaped gardens and ponds and paths, why we buy millions of dollars worth of gardening and home and living simple magazines, is because we long to go back there. To that simple place.

And Creation has been groaning ever since. You don't believe me? Tsunamis, hurricanes, tornadoes, earthquakes, famine, drought, war, murder, disease. I could go on.

But even in the midst of the chaos, God had a plan. Sin requires death as a punishment, because it brings destruction and death and separation. Like in *The Lion, the Witch, and the Wardrobe*. Remember when the great Lion, Aslan dies on the stone table? It was to "satisfy the deep magic." I can sort of understand it, but it's hard, and it's hard to explain. It's like a rule of the universe. Deep magic.

But God sent someone to make it all right again. His son, Jesus, was born as a man, and lived as a man filled with the Holy Spirit. He lived right here physically among us to teach us how it's done. By ourselves we could do nothing, just as Jesus could do nothing on His own. With the Holy Spirit, we can do what He did: heal the sick, raise the dead: clean things up. Help people find their way home. Just like Jesus did. I've heard it said that "Jesus is perfect theology."

And then Jesus died an agonizing death, as a man who had lived a perfect life. He took the sin- He took all the "mad" of God. He took all the anger you see in the Old Testament. He paid for the sin for us, so we wouldn't have to. Because we couldn't. We could die for it, for ourselves, yes, but God wanted more: He wanted us with Him again. The Bible says that we are His joy. And so, Jesus defeated death by rising from it. That smashed the agreement that Adam and Eve had made with Satan. Smashed it to friggin' pieces.

Remember the movie *The Passion*? Remember at the very end, you are looking down on the enemy and he is screaming? That's why he's screaming. He lost.

And now we have a choice. We can choose to give Satan power in our lives by agreeing with him, or we can choose to live like Jesus did, and bring hope and healing to the world. We can choose to look like one of them. We can accuse and blame, and look like Satan and end up representing him on earth. End up adding to the problems and the pain, and becoming part of the problem. Or we can choose to love, and look like Jesus, and fix stuff. We pick up where Jesus left off. We keep cleaning things up. In every way.

I think Christianity is about finding this out about ourselves. Finding that we are not wretches, we are royalty, if we choose to be. Finding out that God is not mad, that He is in a good mood. He is not the author of all the pain. He sent Jesus, who then sent us, to fix it. We were created glorious, like God. There was "original glory" before there was "original sin"! We were not *created* "sinners". We chose that, and God made a way for us to shed that ugly shroud and look like Jesus, if we want to.

And the beauty of it all is we don't have to follow Him or love Him. You don't have to believe me; you don't have to choose Him. But because I have Him living in me, I will always see you as He sees you: beautiful, full of potential, a very much loved son or daughter. I would love to help you know Him. But if you refuse, I still honor you as a child of God, because He does.

So you see -all those hurtful and negative things over the course of your life that you think God did or didn't do? You just found out that it was more the Loki character that did those things to you. He's the real monster in this story. And on top of that, he lied and told you that God did them to you. That's quite a revelation.

So you can keep reading my love story with God, and not worry. I'm not going to try to manipulate or guilt you into anything. I do not believe I can control you, nor do I want to. I only manage me.

He gave me freedom, and I chose to have sex with a guy I didn't know. I could have died, contracted any sort of sexually-transmitted disease, including AIDS. But I got a baby instead. I could have killed this baby, but I didn't. I asked God to help me do the right thing. And now you're reading about how that has played out over the last twenty-three years.

I watch my husband, Phil, with our kids, telling them how smart and beautiful and capable and funny and talented they are, and I know my life would have been different if my dad had told me these things. But I'm thankful that my husband tells me and I'm thankful God always has. And today, my dad tells me. We're all learning to love each other better.

The lies this enemy spoke to me as a child stuck with me until adulthood, and I got so used to them that I didn't even know I believed them. They became my "normal." Looking back, I can see where I heard God, and His encouraging voice, telling me how amazing I was, and who I was, and how loved I was, and I can also see where the enemy lied to me.

By the time I was in high school, I believed the lies more than the truth. And when one believes lies more than truth, one hurts. Partying, alcohol, and messing around with guys were the drugs I chose. There are many things people choose: rage, cruelty, sex, porn, running up credit cards, throwing up their food, manipulating others, lying, video-game addiction, stealing, taking pride in being "perfect" and judging others, to name a few. But whatever they choose to try to comfort or medicate themselves, they hurt themselves, God, and the people around them. Sometimes, the pain gets so great that they murder dozens of people, including children. Whatever it looks like, it's a result of believing lies. It's a result of pain. Some would call that overly-simplified, maybe. I just call it reality.

And so, as I walked to my sister Chris's apartment that day, walking in that pain, I didn't feel the warm sun or the breeze on my face, drying my tears for the moment. She took one look at me and said, "You're pregnant." I had told her of my suspicions a week earlier and she had thought I was overreacting. It was difficult to tell which of us was more miserable.

In those days, my friend Mary stayed with me. She literally stayed with me all day when she wasn't in class and slept over at my house. When I awoke in the middle of the night crying, she would be there. In the morning, when I woke to the darkness choking me and the flood of fear returning, she was there still, speaking words that said that I didn't have to fear, that God would take me through this. Survival seemed unreachable, and she reminded me that I would indeed survive. Basically, every time I believed a lie, she would tell me the truth. Looking ahead at the next nine months, of physically having a baby, of being a mother, paralyzed me. I had to finish college and I had plans for my life and a baby didn't fit. My mom had been a single parent. I had seen how difficult it was. I wanted my baby to have a mother and a father. How could I manage that? This baby's father probably didn't even remember my name. Mary listened to all this over and over, never seeming to run out of patience. She would just look at me with love and empathy. Then she would remind me of the truth, again. I would survive. I wasn't alone. This would turn out well. She was my angel.

My sister Chris and I went for a walk that day, through our campus and town. We talked about motherhood, since I had decided abortion wasn't a choice for us (somehow I knew it wasn't just "me" anymore) and hadn't even thought of adoption. Chris knew that this baby was her niece or nephew, and she wanted me to have him and mother him. She came up with great scenarios: I could have this baby and we could get an apartment together. We'd find jobs with opposite schedules so we could take turns caring for him. Then, I'd meet someone who would want to marry me and father my baby, and everyone would have a happy ending. Perhaps they were a bit fairy-tale-ish, but they eased my load for awhile and gave me hope.

But I still had four parents to tell. Chris went with me to tell Dad. I had no idea how he'd react; this dreadful, empty, gut feeling told me that it would be sickeningly painful. He surprised me. After hearing me out, he simply hugged me and said, "Sometimes daughters make mistakes." My dad reacted just the way God did; how amazing is that?

Today, I am still on a journey of learning to manage myself: my feelings, my appetites, my body, my thoughts. Everything plays into this. How I treat my husband or kids if I'm having an emotionally difficult day. Whether I choose to overindulge in something or choose self-control and take care of myself. Whether or not I choose to hobbit myself and isolate, or get out and serve my community with my gifts.

It all boils down to choosing truth every day instead of lies.

Because I know the truth, and it really does set me free. But I have to choose to believe it, and that's the rub. That's the hard part, "where the rubber meets the road" so to speak. Every single day I get to choose, several times a day, whether I'm going to look like the accuser or look like Jesus.

chapter three

Piglet sidled up to Pooh from behind.
"Pooh," he whispered.
"Yes, Piglet?"
"Nothing," said Piglet, taking Pooh's paw,
"I just wanted to be sure of you."

A.A. Milne, *Winnie-The-Pooh*

May, 1989

As of now, five days later, I've told everyone. My parents, my sisters, my friends, my baby's father. I'm pretty lucky. They've all taken it really well, except my mom. She's having a rough time and she still doesn't talk to me much. It makes me angry; I don't know why she keeps everything inside.

Telling my mom was the most painful: she turned and walked away. I didn't understand. Now I see that when we are overwhelmed by something, we need space to digest. Sometimes we say things we don't mean when confronted and cornered. She was wise. She doesn't react like I do; she waits, she thinks.

My mom saw what was ahead if I chose to parent this child, and she also had friends whose daughters had had children and lived at home. These grandparents had taken on huge parental responsibilities. My mom wasn't going to make that choice. "If you keep it, you don't live here," she had said. At the time I saw that as cruel and thoughtless. I had thought of living at home and parenting. Now I see that she was thinking for both of us. She would not enable me to be completely dependent on her. She knew my lazy tendencies, my immature thinking, my lack of knowledge of what it meant to make house payments. I was an adult, and I needed to take the consequences for my own actions. Hard as it was, she was teaching me to manage myself. I have always thanked her for thinking of not only my best, but my baby's best. Years later, she told me how hard it was for her to give him up as well: he was her first grandchild. Yet, she stood firm. Looking back, I am glad.

It was then that the idea of adoption was planted in my mind. Over the next couple of days, I began to see adoption as a possibility. Not knowing where to turn, I called my pastor and he directed me to an organization called New Life Family Services. When I phoned, they connected me with a social worker named Beth. As soon as I heard her kind voice, the whole story tumbled out. She listened to all my questions, fears, and expectations.

I learned that New Life put their greatest care into the mothers and their babies who went to them for help. They offered post-abortion trauma counseling, help for moms who decided to parent their babies, and adoption services. They wanted to listen. In all my experience with New Life, no one ever tried to tell me what to do. They were simply there to help whether I chose to parent or place for adoption, and to advise me of the realities of abortion or caring for a child. If I chose adoption, I could choose parents myself. I could write them. Someday, I could meet them. Today, a birth mother and adoptive parents can decide on a plan that they are both comfortable with. A birth mother can meet her baby's parents before the baby is born, the parents can even be there for the birth. There have even been instances of a birth mother or father visiting the adoptive family after the adoption has taken place. As for finances, New Life had grants available, and I was eligible for medical assistance, which in the end paid all of my expenses.

Telling my baby's father was uneventful. C. was a year younger than I in college and we had met at a fraternity party. We really didn't know anything about each other; I can't even tell you his major. He was "tall, dark, and handsome," but we didn't have a "night of passion." I've done a lot of things that I am not proud of, and a one-night-stand is one of the most degrading things I have ever chosen to be part of. Alcohol dulled our natural inhibitions and common sense. In fact, most of the stupid things I've done have had alcohol involved. I had that one experience with C., and then hadn't seen him again until I knocked on his dorm room door. I simply told him I was pregnant. He expressed concern for me, and he didn't offer any advice. He just hugged me and said he was sorry.

May 27, 1989

I'm finding that writing in this journal is my release. I know this will be for the good of other women. I'm doing someone some good. God is turning a bad thing into a good thing.

For the most part I feel fine, physically. I keep reminding myself that God is bigger than all of this and He will get me through it. Nine months to me is only a second to Him in the scope of forever.

But that doesn't mean I don't panic. That I don't get the hopeless, terrified feelings. A friend tried to talk me into keeping this baby today. She had a good argument; I'll be too attached, why let a stranger raise my child? She offered to let me live with her and her husband. She had me thinking. Will I always, every day, wonder about this child? Will I regret my decision? Honestly, I don't think so. I feel peaceful about adoption. This baby needs a mom and a dad who love God, and a secure home. New Life is so great, and I know that God is already preparing a couple just for me and my baby. I do have fleeting second thoughts, but I always come back to this.

I had decided to spend my summer waitressing at Naniboujou Lodge, an eight-hour drive north of my home. Since things were tense with my Mom, it was a great diversion for both of us. I spent the first three months of my pregnancy there, living in the staff quarters and waitressing. My room overlooked the lake. My co-workers were supportive and understanding, and Nancy, my boss, was a wealth of information about the physical side of pregnancy. There was one pastor there, working for the summer, who used to tease me about everything. He would catch me in random moments, waiting for the coffee to brew, when I would be rubbing my barely-showing belly. He would laugh and make some joke about how huge I was, or whatever (which I wasn't-

17

yet!) and make me laugh. He listened and wanted to hear my story. It was a wonderful summer. I didn't have much contact with New Life until the fall, when they helped me begin my "parent search."

It was a summer of holding God's hand, "just to be sure of Him." The lake was healing for me. There is something about it: so wide, deep, unfathomable, mysterious, beautiful and dangerous at the same time. It drew me in. It was comforting to be near it. The waves lulled me to sleep and woke me in the morning. I moved my bed directly under my window so I could sleep in the moonlight and wake in the sunlight. I have heard it said that God has two books: The Bible, and Nature. During this time of upheaval, I was drawn to both.

I spent much of my free time walking trails and reading on the beach in the sun. I first discovered *Anne of Green Gables* at the Lodge and was entranced evening after evening, wrapped up in the story of the orphan who had found a beautiful home, family, and adventures. The atmosphere of the Lodge was peaceful, even on the busiest days. And I was certainly in an adventure of my own making.

God kept reminding me of Isaiah 41:10

So do not fear, for I am with you;
do not be dismayed, for I am your God.
I will strengthen you and help you;
I will uphold you with my righteous right hand.

I read this again and again. I had it on slips of paper in my waitressing notebook. It was a constant reminder that I was delighted in, that I was being rescued, that I wasn't alone. He was becoming my hero. Here I was, thinking I was abandoned in a pregnancy, and my lover was with me all the while.

New Life Family Services is still going strong in my state. In fact, just this year, one of our students who attended Bemidji State (BSU) applied for an internship there and asked me to be a reference. I was, gladly. She got the job, and emailed me recently telling me that *The Gift of Sam* is required reading for interns. How cool is that?

I still thank my Mom for making the hard call to force me out of the house. Ian needed a *family*, and I couldn't give him that at that point in my life. Allowing me to live with them would have been enabling me, not empowering me. Not that this is not a viable option for some; I have seen families that embrace grandchildren as their own and make it work.

I try to remember that as my own children reach the age where they need to start managing themselves more. It's so easy to want to bail them out of everything. But a baby eagles wings don't strengthen until the mama pushes them out of the nest, forcing them to fly. My mom forced me to fly. It was one of the best, and the hardest, things she has ever done for me. And when we met Ian three years ago, the first thing he said to me was "thank you."

chapter four

In my mind, I'm where I belong
As I rest in Your arms
And like a child I hold on to You
In my moment of truth, yes I do
We can ride the storm
Endure the pain
You comfort me in my hurricane
And I'll never be alone again

D.C.Talk, *Mind's Eye*

May 28, 1989

When I think about my baby, I think of a small, helpless little person who needs me. I picture him sleeping in my arms and the thought of giving him up makes me nauseous. But then, I remember that I would be caring for him 24 hours a day. Forever. By myself. I can't do that. I don't want to do that.

I want parents for him that will tell him about me and encourage him to find me. All he'll have to do is ask and his parents can give him all the letters I've written them over the years.

God, I need you. Thanks for being so wonderful, for taking care of me through all of this. Thanks for taking me back. Please continue to work on this little baby's father. Let Your will be done in all of this.

I can't ask for anything other than a strong, healthy baby who will grow up to love You. As he grows, please protect him from all the evil in this world; there is so much. Please do for him like You did for me: making Yourself real to me at an early age, taking care of me, loving me. Please, please let his parents be wonderful people. Open, honest, God-loving, rooted, strong people. And please, Lord, let this child want to find me someday.

June 5, 1989

When I arrived last week, Kevin took me out to my favorite place, Pierre's. We talked over pizza and salad...he is an understanding friend and encouraged me to think about the positive things that God is already doing through this. This little life is not a mistake! What my baby's father and I did was wrong, but God is forming this child. He's a miracle. He's about ¾ of an inch long.

It's amazing what I didn't know. In that ¾ of an inch, his little heart was already beating. His eyes were developed, his nervous system all laid out, his ears and nose were forming, his skeleton almost complete, and brain waves could have been recorded. He depended on me to keep him safe and warm. My six-week-old baby was not just a "mass of tissue"; he was a tiny, perfectly formed human being, who would someday be sitting in a public high school thanking me for giving him life.

June 5, 1989

I'm feeling much better physically. Emotionally, I'm doing ok. Beneath all this bustle of activity in my day, I feel this deep loneliness kind of infiltrating. God, I know that You know what I mean. I can't imagine feeling betrayed by You, and that's how You felt: forsaken, forgotten. I know that I'm not. I'm so thankful.

I know that loneliness is part of life, an emotion we deal with. I think like anything else, if we focus on it, it will become who we are. It will become overwhelming. I really believe that my life is driven by the words I speak over it. I'm not a victim. Of anything. I get to choose how I'm going to react to everything that comes my way.

So I know there are legit things that we have to feel, we have to go through them, we have to process them. Like grief. And I know that loneliness can be a part of whatever we're feeling. But I think that it is temporary. We have a sticky note on our refrigerator that says, "Loneliness is a lie not to be believed." Someone said that in a sermon we heard. I know this is true, because I have read stories of people in communist Russia who were imprisoned in the Gulags and thrown into solitary confinement for something horrific like *fourteen years*....and they met God in that prison like you or I maybe never will. And they survived, and came out to tell their stories.

When He says "I will never leave you nor forsake you," He wasn't kidding.

Even in times where I am alone physically and wish I wasn't, I'm not alone. I have the God of the universe living inside of me! I just laughed out loud when I wrote that. Seriously. How can I ever be lonely?

Danny Silk, one of our favorite Bethel Church pastors who has pretty much taught us how to live, said something once that we have never forgotten: When times are tough, get thankful for what I have that is so good. Literally thank God out loud for everything. Then, find someone who is worse off than I am, and bless them somehow. Bless them with the comfort I've received. Then start over, and keep doing this.

I think that so often we run from any kind of pain or discomfort in our lives. And God uses these things to refine us, if we'll let Him. We've already talked about how God doesn't bring this stuff. Pain and suffering come because of the broken community, and because the people who know God are just learning now that they can heal the sick, in more ways than physical. There is no suffering or sickness or disease in heaven, there are none of these things in God. I mean, seriously, what kind of parent would I be if I gave my children sickness to teach them something, to make them better people? I would be arrested for child abuse! And God is an infinitely better parent than I, so why would He? But we make our choices, and they often bring suffering. The beautiful thing is, God can win with any hand.

Think of it this way. I used to have a little home-made natural soap company. It was a blast. (Well, my husband might not agree!) We just made soap with all kinds of wonderful oils and herbs and essential oils, and we used beeswax in our soap. Just a little, to make it harder and so it would last longer. And we made lovely candles from the beeswax as well. Sometimes I would get my beeswax from a bee-keeper in its unrefined form. Have you ever seen unrefined beeswax? It's nasty. It's full of little dead bee parts and dirt and other less-than-desirable cling-ons. So we had to refine it. We would put this huge block of wax in a pot of water and bring it all to a boil. As it all melted in the intense heat, the little dead bee parts and such would float to the top, with the purified wax underneath. Then we would cool the wax and simply slice off the nasty part. Often, we would have to repeat this process one or even two more times, depending on the state the original wax was in. Eventually the wax was clean and sweet-smelling and ready to be used. Then it was melted again for candles or measured out for a batch of soap. I didn't make the wax nasty to begin with. It came to me that way. I just refined it so I could use it to make gorgeous, fabulous smelling soap and candles. But it took a lot of heat and slicing off the bad parts to get it that way.

If we let Him, God will use the heat in our lives to get rid of all the nastiness.

And if we were to stop and consider, what are our choices? When faced with loneliness or pain, what can we do? We can ignore it, surely. Then it would sift itself down into our gut and swill there like nausea, and we would walk around with this vague sense of unrest and illness. We can choose to believe that God doesn't love us. We can reject God and His help and choose to go our own way. Or we can choose faith and trust that God knows what He's doing. We can accept and know that God is in a good mood. He loves us. He likes us. He is glad when He looks at us. We are His "glorious ones, in whom is all His delight." (Psalm 16:3) He made us because He *wanted* to.

We are created to live in freedom and truth. We yearn for beauty because we were created for a garden. In the garden, when God made man, He made us in "His image." We rebel against inconsistency and hypocrisy, because God is consistent and solid. We recoil at injustice because God is just. Deep in our beings we fight to save life because God is life. We spend our days searching for a soul mate because we

23

were created for perfect fellowship with the Lover of our souls. We long for adventure and excitement because God is neither tame nor predictable. We look for simplicity and peace because God clothes the daisies.

Sometimes things like pain and loneliness tempt me with anxiety, but I am not afraid. God will use all things- even pain and grief and loss – to draw us deeper into Him. Yes pain may be a reality in your life right now, but *God is a greater reality.* I find that the quicker I embrace whatever is going on in my life – in the sense that I acknowledge it and talk to God about it and ask Him to give me wisdom about it – the quicker I move past it. He has taught me to reject fear, and to remove it from myself and ask Him to fill that spot. That sounds lofty but it's really just what it says. When I am tempted to be afraid, I say those things, like fear were a person. I reject it. I turn away from it. I tell it that I'm not going to walk with it, because after so many years of being afraid, I refuse to waste one more minute of my life walking with fear. And then I say, "I send you back," like it's a real person, thus removing it from myself. I ask God to forgive me for even considering it, and I ask Him to fill me with His beautiful, peaceful presence. Much of my pain went away when I learned to do this. In fact, I was experiencing panic attacks and a real tightness in my chest, and they influenced each other. If I felt the tightness, I would panic, and vice versa. Once I stood my ground against fear, they disappeared. Once in awhile I am tempted to panic, and I just fight the thing this way.

It's like the movie, *The Lord of the Rings: The Return of the King*. There is a scene where Eowyn, neice of King Theoden, has disguised herself as a man in order to fight alongside her countrymen against the dark lord Sauron's demonic troops. Their leader, the Witch-King, perched upon his Nazgul-dragon, swoops down and throws King Theoden, trapping him under his dead horse. Then the beast and the Witch King land in front of him, and the beast is ordered to "feast on his flesh." But Eowyn steps between them, dressed as a man, helmet on her head, sword in her hand, and she says, "I will *kill* you if you touch him!" The scene is shot from behind her, and you see this small, thin woman in armor with her sword raised and a huge dragon-like beast, fangs bared, in front of her.

The uber-creepy voice says, "Do not come between the Nazgul and his prey." The dragon takes a swipe, fangs bared, at Eowyn.

So she does what every good mom would do: she swings her sword and hacks off the dragon's head. The Witch King dismounts his now-dead dragon, faces Eowyn, and says, "You fool. No man can kill me." Then he starts swinging at her with what looks like a cannonball with spikes attached to a chain. He shatters her shield, and grabs her by the throat, lifting her up off the ground.

"Die" he hisses.

Right when it looks like all is lost, her friend Merry stabs the Witch King in the calf with his dagger. Eowyn, released from his grasp, whips off her helmet and says, "I am no man."

She then, uh, *dispatches* the Witch King. Something no man is supposed to be able to do. But apparently a woman can.

I love that scene. I have found a picture of it and have taped it to the wall in front of my desk. It reminds me of what I am doing, every day of my life, for myself, my husband, my children, and our students. I am the one between us and the beast. I am the one who will cut off its head with my prayers and words. I can't quit, even when it feels like the thing has got me by the throat, hissing its intimidation. The dragons of loneliness, suicide, fear, despair, self-pity, self-loathing have their heads regularly hacked off in my world.

Maybe through this book I can do that with you. My hope is that you will see what God has done for me and begin to find the same beauty in every area of your life. And kill a few dragons of your own.

We are continually dealing with broken spots in our lives. In campus ministry, Phil and I have seen that we are basically a culture of orphans: they try to live life themselves, by themselves. My husband leads a men's group that consists of a bunch of guys who have never been taught to be "sons," meaning that whenever they felt pain, they didn't know what to do with it and they didn't know how to ask for help or who to ask. So they simply medicated themselves. Video games, sex, porn, alcohol, drug use – anything can be a false comforter.

If you think about it, they've been doing this their whole lives. I see our little son, Eli, who is nine as I write this. He was having a really rough time at school a year ago. He had a run-in with his gym teacher, and hearing him tell it, it sounded to me like the gym teacher had a bad day and took it out on the kids. So I went in to talk to her, and frankly, I didn't keep my cool. Several times have I listened to Eli talk about how he was reduced to tears in gym class, and told to stop crying "like a big boy." I see too many young adults who have been taught their whole lives to stuff their feelings and emotions. And I see them now, unable to control themselves in the addictions they've gotten themselves into, trying to medicate their pain that they can't even name because they've been told to stuff it and not deal with it.

I heard her side of the story, and I understood a little better. I still don't agree with how she handled it, but I left her reconciled, although still unaware as to why Eli was having this pain.

About a week later, Eli asked if he could talk to me. He began to tell me about how he and his friends were playing a game on the playground that was becoming spiritually and emotionally unhealthy. Most people might look at it as nothing, but to him, it was a big deal, and it had been weighing on his heart. It was causing him grief and guilt. So I helped him to forgive himself, forgive whomever else he needed to forgive, and ask God to forgive him for doing something against his conscience. It didn't seem like a big deal, truly. But from that point on, whenever his "heart hurts" he comes to talk to me, and we deal with it. We find what it was that hurt him, we help him forgive those people or himself, and we have him ask God for the truth about the situation. And every so often, we ask him how is heart is feeling.

But immediately, we had a different kid. We had our happy Eli back. No more crying in gym class, no more sadness that lingered and worried us. He was a carefree kid again. We haven't had another issue with the gym teacher or any teacher.

And it's got me thinking. If you don't have a parent or guardian or adult in your life who helps you deal with stuff "when your heart hurts," what do you do? I suppose you medicate yourself, you comfort yourself however you can. Video games are a big one. If you are introduced to porn, that can become a terrible debilitating addiction. The list goes on. But I see these guys in Phil's group as guys who were never taught what to do when their "hearts hurt" as a child. Have you ever heard or seen that quote that has been going around on Facebook, the one that says "It's easier to build up a child than repair an adult"? I don't think it's true, and I think it is a hopeless statement. Building up a child is awesome. But I've seen God do some pretty astonishing repair on adults.

And the guys in Phil's group are becoming powerful men of God. Every week my husband comes home and says, "I am so proud of these guys." He's proud of them because they are learning to deal with their feelings and their hurt in powerful ways. They are learning to talk to other guys, to name how they are feeling, to forgive immediately, to see and call out the best in each other, and to live by the truth of who God says they are. They don't wallow in self-pity or depression or rage or fear. They are learning that their words set the course of their lives.

This is what he tells them: pain is our friend. It is simply a warning light on our dashboard, telling us that something is broken and needs to be fixed. These guys are learning to not be afraid of pain, find the broken spots, and get them fixed. And they are rising up and becoming an army that I would not want to be on the other side of.

These are not weak men. These are men who are learning that they are strong, and they are learning to use that strength.

I am writing a companion to this book, a guided journal to help you work through your own pain. We will go into greater detail there as to how to go about it. Until then, journal it. Forgive it, ask God for the truth about it. He will help fix the broken spots.

chapter five

"Jesus?" he whispered as his voice choked "I feel so lost."

A hand reached out and squeezed his, and didn't let go. "I know Mack.
But it's not true. I am with you and I'm not lost. I'm sorry it feels that
way, but hear me clearly.
You are not lost."

William Paul Young, *The Shack*

June 19, 1989

Sometimes when I sit and really think about it, this wave of
darkness crashes down. All around me the birds are singing and the
sky is deep blue and the sun is bright...it is one of those perfect
North Shore days. It's times like this that I feel cheated: like I
should be as carefree as the waves.

But then, I force myself to remember the night that all the
northern lights lit up the sky and God said, "Look, Michelle. See
what I do. I command the sky to bring beauty like this. I am bigger
than you. I can handle your life.

If I just calm my spirit for awhile from all the giddiness of daily
life and look and see what God has done, if I take the time to ingest
His promises, I see that He is in control.

God, take my heart. You understand me, you know what I need. Please help me because I want to be entirely yours…I really do. But I know myself. I remember how many times I've fallen backwards. I know how much I enjoy "sin" and the lifestyle it brings. Lord, I just have to trust that you'll bring wonderful things. I know, even though I don't always feel, that if I seek You, You will show me. Please help me never to stop seeking. I want to love You, Lord.

I love how I was always talking myself out of feeling the way I knew wasn't true. I would get close to the edge of self-pity or despair in my journals, and then start telling myself the truth, therefore pulling myself up out of the pit. Journaling is so good. I can see God talking to me, influencing me, all over these. And I can see who I am today, starting to show itself even back then -which is incredibly encouraging, two decades later.

June 20, 1989
Nine weeks

I have to remember that this baby is God's, not mine. Sure, he's coming from me, but God allowed him to happen, not me. He's forming him, He knows his little personality, He knows all the days of his life. He's a wanted child. He will touch a lot of lives. It took something like this to knock some sense back into me. I had all the right words for Christianity, but none of it was in my heart. It didn't come out in my actions.

Except now I don't believe that "this baby was God's, not mine." He *was* mine. I needed to take responsibility for him, give him the best I could give. And I did. God didn't "take over" and force me to do anything. He taught me to live my faith as well as talk about it. It came to a place where I had to face it. And He empowered me. So you'll see some of that in these old journals, but my thinking has changed.

August 29, 1989

Little baby, you are getting so big. Starting about a week ago, I can feel you all the time. It's getting harder to get out of bed, because my muscles are all stretched over you and they're not working as well. I'm finding I have to use my arms and legs more.

I hope you love me someday. I hope your parents are the kind of people who tell you every day how much I love you and want to be part of your life when you're ready. But I know that giving you to them is the right thing to do, for us. I am choosing to believe that God has the best parents in the world picked out for you. I want them to raise you like I wish I could, so we're probably a lot alike. They're just older and wiser and more settled than I am.

I think I freaked you out when I sneezed just now. You kind of rumbled, like I woke you up or something. You've been nudging me, too. It feels like your little feet are about an inch long. You're probably laughing at that now; if you're like your father at all you'll be big and tall.

You know, I never saw you as a mistake. Never. What your dad and I did was a mistake, giving part of ourselves away like that. Violating God's laws that are there to protect us. It only brought us pain. But you...you are the blessing that Jesus brought me even when I was walking away from Him. He brought you: a joy to me and a joy to your parents.

Don't worry, I don't expect you to be perfect. You may not even see things the way I do. I hope you're not angry with me. Because of you, I am back to everything that means something to me. One reason you came was to help your mom get her life together and grow up a little. Through having you, I see that with God all things are possible. Yes, I am giving part of myself to your parents when I give them you. But you are a gift I was never meant to keep. Be glad, baby. God has already used you more than you know.

So you see, you are special. In God's eyes, you were planned. I remember asking God one day, when I knew my life was headed down the wrong path, to do whatever He had to. I didn't want to come back to Him , but I wanted to *want* to. Do you know what I mean? He granted that prayer with you. You were not a mistake, and you will never be seen as one.

After all that God has done for me through you, I could never keep you and force you to live the kind of life we would have. Not that we wouldn't love each other, but it just wouldn't be the best. You deserve a daddy. You wouldn't have one with me. You would be stuck in day care all the time, being raised by people I don't know. Oh, baby, I can't do it. I want you to have a mommy and a daddy. Then, when you're ready, you can have me, too. I'll let you grow up in their love first. But I will miss you. I'll miss you so much.

God has answered most of these prayers you just read. He has brought wonderful things. I am married to an incredibly hard working, sensitive, faithful, selfless man. He wouldn't say that, and he would probably be embarrassed by my saying that, but it's true. He has his moments, and he's not perfect, but I cannot imagine being married to anyone else in the entire world. He is perfect for me, and vice versa. And we started out rough, really rough, as you will see. But God is faithful, specializing in those who cannot help themselves, and here we are.

And I have never regretted giving him a family. After I married Phil, God gave us three little girls within the first six years of our marriage. This was wonderful! Seven years after that, we had Eli, and once I had another little boy in my arms, I began to realize what I had missed with Ian. I grieved him again, but not in a painful way: in a bittersweet way. I still wanted the best for him, and he had it. I still had no intention of ever intruding on his life until he asked for me, because I believed, and still believe, that I did the best for him. I somehow knew and trusted that God would bring him back to me, and to his step-father and his sisters and his brother, when he was ready.

And I laugh as I read this! There is a joy of hopes fulfilled that I can't even describe to you. I have never regretted giving him a family. And now, having him part of our lives, it just makes me laugh when I read all the hopes I had twenty-three years ago. They have all happened! I *hoped* his parents would tell him about me - that I wanted to be part of his life - and they did. They did, all during his growing up. I *hoped* that he would have the "best parents in the world." He has told me since, and thanked me, for choosing them. His growing up experience was full of love and fun and learning, happily. I *hoped* they would raise him like I would, and I find myself now, raising our three girls and Elijah with Kiki's words in my head….. "acceptance to be the little person they were created to be…" I know this is my story, but even reading it again, when it's *my life*- I am overwhelmed with the ravishing goodness of God. I can hardly believe how it has all turned out.

Once we were reunited, and I will tell you that story, I asked him: Did you ever feel abandoned? Were you ever angry with me? His immediate and determined answer was "No. Never." When I asked how that could be, he said, "Well, when I would think of it, I would dismiss it, because I thought, 'I don't know anything about that, so.'" It was like our God just put a protective barrier around his heart and mind concerning me and the circumstances of his birth. It still shakes the awe in me. Even my words, "when you're ready, you can have me too," happened. He was ready. Now we run triathlons together.

He's getting married this summer. In Dallas. I get to buy a great dress. And I'm still laughing, all the time.

chapter six

from the place where morning gathers
you can look sometimes forever til you see
what time may never know
what time may never know
how the Lord takes by its corners this old world
and shakes us forward and shakes us free
to run wild with the hope
run wild with the hope

the hope that this thirst will not last long
that it will soon drown in a song
not sung in vain
I feel the thunder in the sky
I see the sky about to rain
And I hear the prairies calling out your name

Rich Mullins, *Calling Out Your Name*

At the end of August, 1989, my summer job was over and I packed up and headed back home. I didn't want to leave; the North Shore felt like my home, and my time there was like a honeymoon with God. But I was looking forward to a future weekend trip up with my friends. And so you move from hope to hope.

I started school, taking my last two literature classes. My professors and fellow students were heartening. I came to class one day and found a flower on my chair, from a friend who "just wanted to see me smile a little." Later, he told me that a former girlfriend had aborted their baby, and it was still painful for him. He was proud of me for allowing my child to live. I was so touched by the gesture.

During this time, I started searching for "the perfect parents." I filled out a form outlining what qualities I was looking for in parents for my baby. Then Beth and the adoption worker, Anne, matched up my requirements with those couples who seemed to fit best. Next, I received these "summaries" three at a time to look over. They all had code names: MT, AR, PQ, etc. The summary detailed things like parenting and education philosophies, type of home they lived in, their church and hobbies, each spouse's description of the other spouse, and minors like nationality and physical characteristics. I had this choice narrowed down to two, although they didn't seem to be exactly what I was looking for. Then Beth called me and said they had one more for me to look at: a couple who had just been returned to the pool because the girl who had chosen them had changed her mind at the last minute and decided to parent. This couple, called XL, had been chosen and disappointed three times in the course of seven months.

As written to me by Beth, "Because this couple is such a prayer-warrior couple, they always crucified their will for the girl and baby's best. The family always trusted God that those babies were closed doors. It showed maturity, guts, and faith to work through it without self-pity or resentment."

That hooked me. They were everything I was looking for. They were mature, open, honest, down-to-earth. They weren't afraid that I would come back and take my baby away from them. They trusted that God had a plan for them, no matter what came.

I was looking for a couple who would take a girl or a boy, perfect or imperfect. I didn't want my baby sitting in foster care, rejected because he didn't have all his fingers or toes. I wanted them to love my baby like they would love their own: not knowing if they would have a boy or girl, or whether he or she would be completely healthy, with all fingers and toes, so to speak. I wanted them to love my baby as much as I did, *right now*. And I wanted them to love me, because we would be a family. I hoped to be part of their lives someday.

I had a friend who was adopted, and when she started thinking of finding her birth mother, her adoptive family put her through all kinds of guilt. I didn't want my baby's parents to be the kind of people who would say, "Aren't we enough for you?" when he was ready to find me. I wanted them to encourage him to find me, because they knew me and

34

knew his life would be richer for it. Because they weren't insecure or afraid. We are all family in God's kingdom anyway. I carried him, I bore him, they would raise him. They would be his parents, and I would always be his birth mother.

Don and Kiki are the best. They were everything I was looking for. They had, and still have, a strong marriage, and they are still married after countless fertility tests and disappointed near-adoptions. "My parents" turned to God for their strength in the midst of circumstances that could tear apart a marriage, or at least make for a bitter one. They knew God had a perfect plan – or could make one out of whatever He was handed – and they rested in that.

September 15, 1989
5 ½ months

Giving up my baby is starting to become real to me now. Not that I'm thinking of changing my mind. This baby is God's.

He is with me everywhere. He and I are always doing things together. Like my relationship with God, I can't see him but I know he's there. I only hope that his parents tell him about me. I don't want to be a closed case after we leave the hospital.

Then I think about how happy this couple will be. I only pray they remember me. I hope they can satisfy his little mind: I want him to understand why I'm doing this.

I just realized that when I kept saying "This baby is God's, not mine" maybe what was going on in my heart was that I had dedicated him to the Lord already, before he was even born. I had so committed my course to Him, knowing He had an infinitely better idea of where it should all end up than me, that in my mind, Ian was more God's baby than mine. I still took responsibility; I still did my best for him. I just truly believed that he wasn't only mine. Like God was the father in this scenario, and deserved a say.

It was really important to me that the parents love me as well as my baby. I expressed that same hope over and over. I thought I had chosen the best parents I could; I had no second thoughts, but still the nagging insecurities reared up at times. I think this is what I meant when I wrote that "it was starting to become real to me." I had to keep going back to what I knew was true. This baby was a gift. This situation was being used to grow me into a deeper relationship with God and therefore to grow me as a person. I would come out of this stronger than I went in. It would hurt. But God promised to walk with me and strengthen me and help me. He would help me find my path again.

The adoption horror stories did scare me, and at times Don and Kiki seemed too good to be true. But isn't God too good to be true? Yet He is all He says He is. We can't comprehend all at once the greatness of Him and His love for us. The universe cannot contain Him. But one day, we will see Him face to face, and "we will be like Him, for we shall see Him as He is." (1 John 3:2) This is unfathomable. At that time I needed to just let go of my fear and believe that something was as good as it seemed. That was really frightening, but I was able to believe that X and L were who they said they were. Realistically, God held my baby; not people. Not me, not them.

I expressed my concerns to Beth, my social worker at New Life. One way they helped me with all this was to give me an Advocate: a volunteer who met with me usually once a week just to talk. Mine was Pam. She was a mother of seven and a pastor's wife. We met once a week at a little diner half-way between our homes. She would send me bright and hopeful notes during the week. She prayed. I talked and talked and had a million questions about family, marriage, the upcoming birth, and parenting. She was rather quiet and introverted, but she answered my exuberant questions as well as she could. She directed me to keep looking to God, who wouldn't lead me into something that would break my heart. She continually reminded me of the Father's great tenderness. She never tried to tell me what to do, she trusted that my decision in the end would be the best. That was incredibly valuable to me. I never felt pushed, in any way.

Before I knew it, the time had come for my long-awaited weekend on the North Shore. It had been only five weeks since I left, but it seemed longer. School was going well, I had chosen my parents, and overall, I was feeling good. Things with my mom were better. I think the time away helped her as well; she could deal with me and my growing pregnancy more easily. She was also happy with my adoption decision, although she knew it would be difficult, for all of us. This would be the first grandchild.

My college friends Mary and Meg and I rented a tiny little cabin right on Lake Superior, about a mile from the Lodge. We had a wonderful time. We hiked, hung out at the Lodge, took pictures, shopped, and spent many hours just talking. It felt so good to breathe the pine-scented air again and to sit and ponder Lake Superior. The breezes off the lake were restful. I have a deep respect for this lake. It is beautiful, and it is good, but it isn't safe. Kind of like when Mr. Beaver tells Lucy about Aslan in *The Lion, The Witch, and the Wardrobe*:

"Safe?" said Mr. Beaver; "don't you hear what Mrs. Beaver tells you? Who said anything about safe? 'Course he isn't safe. But he's good. He's the King, I tell you."

Something about that, in spite of it, makes me feel safe.

September 23, 1989
Six months

Baby, I wonder if you can hear the waves crashing up our cobblestone beach, or the steaming of the gas stove that's keeping my feet warm. Do you feel the same contentment that I do here? I'll be curious to know. I'll remember these things: where we spent our time, who with, what we said. It will be so strange to be just me again after you're born, after you leave. Even though it's just you and I here, your parents are at this moment in my mind and they don't even know us yet! Since God knows them, and in that sense has joined us all together, I feel like I'm sharing you now. That you were never just "mine."

I hope you realize how much I love you. You are such a part of me. A lot of people say I'm doing such a loving thing, giving you up. Unselfish. But I've thought about it a lot and I don't think that's one hundred percent true. Either way, I'm being both selfish and unselfish. It's unselfish because some could say that I'm only thinking of you and not of my pain. To raise you I would sacrifice, and that would be unselfish. But keeping you could be seen as selfish

because I couldn't bear to be without you. Giving you up because I want my own life could be seen as selfish. See what I mean?

It doesn't matter. I thought and talked and thought and cried and prayed until I felt comfortable with a decision. It was a decision made by me. I really am doing my best.

Someday, I would like to come here with you. I'd like to show you all the things I love and see if you love them, too. Dark, starry skies, northern lights, Superior's waves, the smells of clean air and pine. We will sit here, all of our families together, and catch up. I look forward to just watching you.

Well, baby, before you decide to wake up and start kick boxing me, I'm going to sleep. So I won't notice when you do. Do you know that you have the worst timing? First, you never kick in front of anyone else when I want you to, and second, you either kick during class, which is distracting, or when I am trying to fall asleep, which is obnoxious! I love you, Baby!

I vividly remember writing this, sitting in front of that little gas stove that was hissing away, warming my toes. My friends had gone to sleep, and I was up, writing by the firelight. It was one of those peace-and-contentment-filled moments that we always remember. I see it now when one of our kids is lying on the couch with Phil, or snuggled with him in our "person-and-a-half" sized chair. That safety of being in Daddy's arms. It's such a beautiful place to be.

Last summer, Ian joined us in the Trinona. He thanked me for making him feel like a sloth the previous summer when he and his family came to watch and cheer. That made me laugh, he's such a funny guy. So he trained for the next summer, and we all competed together. It was what you would expect: a blast.

After the race, we all descended on Don and Kiki's (X and L) house for a couple days. I believe it was when Ian was a teenager that we exchanged phone numbers and I learned their names. It is funny now to call them "X and L," but we all do it from time to time. Better yet, I still call Kiki "Lollipop" sometimes, because that's exactly her personality!

Don and Kiki have a beautiful home in a suburb of Minneapolis, with a pool and hot tub in the back yard. Kiki and I were in the hot tub, and the rest of the family was playing and running and having a blast. It's in these moments, when it's just her and I that she'll look at me.....and growl.

Yes, and it's hilarious! She has this "happy Kiki growl" that comes out....I can't describe it. Then she will say something like, "that FACE!!" (meaning me) "I love that FACE!"

To which I will reply, "Of course you do. You've been looking at it for twenty three years!"

Ian got engaged a few months after that. I got one of the "call the parents" phone calls after he proposed. Since then, plans are being made for a wedding at a beautiful garden in Dallas, the home-town of his Chaley. She's a lovely young woman; we all adore her! After the wedding, there are plans to have a MN reception at some point. I gave Kiki the offer of my help, in any way, and she said, "Yes, woman! We're in this together, you and I!"

We're the mamas. It's a beautiful thing. My hope that I wouldn't be a "closed case" after leaving the hospital so many years ago, has been fulfilled, and is continually being fulfilled. I am a mother of the groom. We are running another triathlon this summer. I will soon have a daughter-in-law.

All my hopes that "we would come here together someday" have happened. We spent a weekend together in Duluth, all of us. We pondered Superior's waves and skipped rocks and buried ourselves in the sand. I've gotten to "just watch him" many, many times. It's so fun. He's so much like all of us, in so many ways. Goofy mannerisms, gestures, facial expressions. He was never just mine, but he is so obviously mine, at the same time.

chapter seven

"I don't need to punish people for sin. Sin is its own punishment,
devouring you from the inside. It's not my purpose to punish it; it's my
joy to cure it."

William Paul Young, *The Shack*.

October 4, 1989

Dear Lord, my life is so good. It sounds so simple, but "thank you." I know there are people who love me. School is almost finished. Money is tight, but it's there. I'm giving a beautiful baby to a waiting couple. The reality of what I barely missed (AIDS, STD's, abortion, rape) overwhelms me. I don't know how to thank You for such gifts. I love you, Jesus. Please make me like You. Teach me to love. Thank you for loving my baby. I need you, Lord; I would die without You.

I can't tell you, baby, how much you mean to me: you are such a part of me that the thought of losing you seems unbearable. But I know your little body and spirit need love and care. You won't recognize who is giving that love and care for the first six weeks or so. You won't miss me; you won't feel a loss. That is not your fault: none of this is your fault.

I want you to have a mom and a dad. With me you won't. You would grow up confused with a confused father, in and out of your life. He was cited for public nuisance the other night. I wish I could help him; for your sake I'll keep trying. I will do my best to forgive him and love him and be a real friend to him so I can tell you in all

honesty when you ask me: we are friends. He's not a bad man, baby. He's just young, and has done some stupid things like me.

Me, who wants to be a full-time mom for you. But how could I do that? We could live on welfare, but then where would we go? I could find a job and put you in daycare all day. Why? Why not give you a mom and dad?

I'm not the only one losing you. Your grandparents, your aunts: this is hard for them, too. They don't really talk about it with me. Everyone waits for the first grandchild, and you're it.

I wonder what kind of person I must be to give you up. Will you hate me someday, or worse, not care at all? Will you understand? I pray you will. I feel this bond we have, and I pray it will stay rooted in your heart always.

October 18, 1989
Six ½ months

It feels so good to cry. I've been holding everything in lately. I feel like I've become this hardened mass of rock and flesh. Pam keeps telling me that my emotions are wild when pregnant. I can't help feeling that I'm abnormal, unfeeling, apathetic. She said that her toughest times were when she was pregnant. I believe her. I've shut everyone out except those closest to me, those I'm completely comfortable with. And even my family doesn't understand my faith. I wish they knew.

I don't like people touching me: you know, patting my middle and asking "how's baby?" Meg did that the other day and I barked at her. I feel bad, now, of course. She was only wondering. I don't even like going to church because I am tired of being strong, answering people's questions. Do they really want to know how I'm doing? It's not that I don't believe my answers...all this happened for a reason, God has a plan, my baby is getting the best I can give...I believe these things. I know God loves me and has a perfect plan. But I feel so lousy.

Sometimes I am afraid, still. I'm such a wimp when it comes to pain, and having a baby is painful. Can I go through with this? I have to. I get so angry sometimes when I think of my baby's father and how he doesn't have to deal with any of this. He chose to walk away. Sometimes I think I hate him; I find myself wanting to see him hurt. I'm not going to tell him when our baby is born. Let him wonder.

I pray often for God to help me through. I just want to be normal again. I can't imagine being without my baby; I can't imagine ever being the same again. What have I done?

November 10, 1989

I just found a centipede in my *bed,* and to me that is the grossest thing in the world. Well, maybe second, only to writing my Victorian Lit. paper. I'm lost.

When I marry and have children, at least I'll be able to warn my husband about how irritable I get. I've nearly abused our poor cat to death...he keeps getting into the garbage and climbing on counters. I almost caught myself picking him up by the *neck* today – good Lord, am I that violent? Pam says it's normal. I hope the humane society doesn't find out how normal I am.

Sometimes I wonder what it must be like to adopt a baby. Wow. To be able to have a child and not be recovering from the trauma of birth or a long pregnancy. To be strong and rested and healthy when you start parenting. Don't get me wrong, pregnancy can be a wonderful experience. But it would be amazing to get a baby and not have just come off of nine months of upheaval!

Hormones really do affect our thinking sometimes. The feelings I was experiencing *were* normal: I was in a crisis situation. I mean, who thinks of these things in a normal, day-to-day existence? I had choices to make and uphold that would determine the outcome of someone else's life. That is a sober responsibility for anyone, even in a happily wed, two-parent family. I know now that I can choose my thoughts: I can "take every thought captive and make it obedient to Christ," (2 Corinthians 10: 5) but that took time to learn and practice. Even then, hormones and huge life decisions can make things...strained, sometimes. I tell pregnant moms this all the time now. Give yourself a break. Get your head on straight in the morning, tell yourself the truth, let God tell you the truth, and wage that war one day at a time.

And take lots of breathers, with your feet up and a nice cup of mint tea.

Remember that movie *Parent Trap*? I used to love that movie when I was a kid. I couldn't have told you why. Then a friend said something to me about how it made sense that I loved it, because it would have been my dream that my parents would get back together.

Thinking about it now, I don't think that was it. I think it was the *idea* of two people loving each other, through the good and bad. It was the dream of how things should be, in a perfect world. That's all.

I don't think anyone would argue that dads are important. And I just wanted him to have one. I think it was the dream of giving Ian something I never had, and the dream that I would someday have a marriage that would work. I didn't have that at the moment he was born, so I chose to give him the best I could. Furthermore, I had no idea what to expect of this baby's father. Would he be in our child's life? Out? Wavering? What about his family? Would they want to see Ian? What would I do if they challenged my parenting and wanted him? I believed that God had someone for me, and I could risk my own happiness on that; plan my own life for that. I could not risk his.

And to be completely honest, I just wasn't ready to parent. I knew it.

November 7, 1989

Re-reading this journal has a sort of healing effect on me. In some ways it's funny how confused I have been...never about the *facts*, just about my feelings. It's like I always know the bottom line: giving you, Baby, to your parents is the right thing for everyone. But

my emotions are constantly swinging! I'm grateful that the solid foundation will always be there and will always be true.

I still have emotional roller coaster days today, but they are much fewer and further in between. I have learned, thank God, how to choose the truth. If I'm feeling crabby, I know that being crabby is not my nature. So I tell crabbiness to take a hike and I release joy over myself. Jesus lives in me. He is joy, therefore I have it in me to release. But it has to be deliberate sometimes, most times. Today I have solutions, and I have tools. I will talk about them much more in the journal companion to this book, but suffice it to say, I set the course of my life with my words. Even today, I have to remember this every day. Tell myself the truth. God's word tells me who I am and who He is. Those are the things that are true, no matter how I feel.

And can I say, do I even need to say, that Ian never once felt hatred towards me, as my journals feared? He loves us, and he cares a great deal. When he can, he comes for weekends. We have a great time, playing games and hanging out. It is hilarious to hear him and his sisters and brother play Halo. It's almost more fun to listen to them play than to play, in my opinion!

Reading and experiencing all this again has brought many thoughts to mind. One is that when we are in crisis, I wonder, is it kind of like "fasting lukewarm-ness?" Fasting happens all over the world in many different cultures and religions. We "fast" or deprive ourselves of something for a period of time, to clarify our thinking or clear a channel with God. Looking back, every time I had a crisis in my life, I automatically kicked into fasting mode. I fasted lukewarm-ness towards God. I got desperate for Him.

I know that God doesn't bring chaos or pain or trial, but He allows it. I really believe that the enemy is the author of pain, not God. But God takes the enemy's dark strands and weaves them through our lives to bring out the color, to provide contrast and depth to our lives. He's a genius.

I made a choice twenty-four years ago that altered the course of my life, and it has never been the same. It has been better. I can't imagine life without Ian and his family, my family. It's been, and still is, an adventure I would have never wanted to miss. The "dark strands," when

44

seen on the finished side of the tapestry, don't look dark anymore. They transform to something much lighter and lovelier.

chapter eight

I was born where the rivers run
Native blood runs through my veins
I was born where the eagles come
Waiting till the winter fades

I was born an endangered son
I was spared by a mother's dream
I was saved by the power of love
I was snatched from the fire of greed

Great river road where justice rolled
Let it roll, let it roll down
Great river road where healing flowed
Let it flow, let it flow now

I was born to an orphaned son
I was seed from a broken life
I was just like the other ones
Waiting on the other side

I was born because freedom won
Mother sent me down the stream
I was saved by the power of love
I was snatched from the fire of greed

Jason Upton, "Great River Road"

From early on in my pregnancy, I believed my baby was a boy. I
don't know why, it was just that I couldn't imagine he was a girl. I had a

name chosen: Samuel Carson. Carson after a dear friend, and Samuel, I don't know. It just came to me: it just felt right.

October 23, 1989

I realize now what the Lord is telling me.

I am like Hannah. In some ways, I asked for this child. I knew my life was going wrong, and I prayed that God would do what He had to to make it right. So He gave me a baby to carry for nine months, to mother for a few days, and to give back to Him to care for his entire life. I may never see this child again. I may never have another. Hannah prayed for a son, and God remembered her. Then she gave him up. She trusted God with her son: Samuel.

I decided to name my baby Samuel before I knew this story. This is a huge confirmation that I am doing the right thing! Lord God, please continue to teach me to trust!

This revelation hit me like a flood. I had a vague recollection in my mind about the Biblical story of Hannah but I couldn't remember the name of her child. The story kept coming up in my thoughts, until finally I looked it up, in the parking lot of the clinic after one of my prenatal visits. Then, the doors of my mind were flung open and all of a sudden it made sense. Hannah named her son Samuel. My son's name would be Samuel. I had chosen that name months ago. She gave her son to God. I was giving my son to God to care for. The parallels between her story and mine astounded me. It was so beautiful; that I would choose a name seemingly for no reason, and then months later God would show me the meaning of the name and it fit perfectly. God, the creator of the universe, had been thinking of me. He had my baby in His mind. With all the ravages of the world: famine, plague, murder, strife, hatred... He had time to think of me. A connection or "confirmation" like that gave me confidence to move forward.

It was like thinking I might be lost in the woods and all of a sudden finding that I was on the right trail after all.

It was time to begin writing "my parents." It was so exciting that I could put personalities to code letters; that I could actually get to know

47

them before "our" baby was born. Today, things are much more open; in fact, they are as open as a birth mother and adoptive parents want them to be. My sister and brother-in-law have even taken the birth mother of their daughter on vacations with them. It's so much about *family,* and about giving a child the best you can, rather than holding on. How much would change if we all started seeing each other, even strangers, as family?

Here are our letters.

December 21, 1989

Dear XL,

I am writing this before our baby is born. I realize that this may be a bit frightening for you, thinking that you may get let down. But I can honestly tell you that I know this is God's decision for us. By communicating with you now, I am being assured that this precious child doing somersaults inside me right now is going into loving, capable hands. Being that God led me specifically to you and seemingly vice versa, I should have no need for reassurance. Just human, I guess, huh? I've read and heard the horror stories and I let them get to me probably just like everyone else. I don't believe I've ever been this concerned about someone else's welfare. This baby has taught me a lot. I have never had to make a sacrifice or choose whether to let someone live or die. I praise God that He helped me to make the right choice.

There are many thoughts that have held me to my decision. One was knowing that above all the confusion and pain I have sometimes felt, that this is God's plan for us. Another was imagining the joy I would be giving to you. How does that feel? What do you want to know about me? I want to share everything: I wish I could sit down with you and tell you the whole story from the beginning. I wish you could be there when our baby is born; I wish I could give him to you myself.

It's hard to imagine my baby growing up without me; knowing two other people as mom and dad. But I know it's for the best.

48

According to Anne and Beth, I've been given a "one in a million couple" and I can't tell you how good that makes me feel.

There are so many things I want to say and I feel like part of them have come out in a jumbled mess in this letter. I'll stop here and wait to hear from you. Thank you for being the people that you are. Take care.

Your birth mom

January 3, 1990
Dear Birth mom,

Thanks so much for your wonderful letter! For the sake of our writing, we'll refer to husband as "X" and wife as "L." Wow, sounds a little impersonal! One of X's first comments while reading your letter was "she sounds a lot like you!" We agree that God has been and is leading us together. Your "need for assurance" is wonderful. God has given us each a heart and mind to use to His glory. When we have questions, the Lord wants to know them and desires us to seek Him and His strength. Your heart and relationship with the Lord is encouraging to us. We are grateful that you are desiring to seek the Lord's direction. While the world eagerly pushes the "easy way out" of such a situation, it takes courage to face the issue and make responsible decisions. We thank God for you and your love for Him.

We have waited for the day when a little person will be in our arms. The joy you will be giving us is beyond words; more than we can ask or think! One of our highest desires in life is to raise a little person, in a home filled with God's love, having that little heart and mind grow knowing that they are a wonderful person and thoroughly loved!

We want to be sensitive to a little person growing up knowing they're adopted and be able to fill in as much of the unknown part of

49

their life as possible. You are and always will be important to us and "our" child.

What do we want to know about you? Where do we begin? We look at your letter and see the handwriting and composition of someone who's neat, organized, sensitive, loving, caring, creative! Sounds like we're analyzing your handwriting! It's strange when it's all we've got.

We're interested in who you are; what kind of environment did you grow up in, what things helped shape the person you are, what kind of person do you see yourself as? Anne has briefly shared some of your interests. We'd love to hear more! Who you are is going to be so much a part of our little person.

We both grew up in Christian homes where God and His love were the highest priority. We are from the same evangelical denominational background and met in early college days. I thank God often for our upbringing. Our families have similar lifestyles and goals. What we came from is a lot of who we are. Both families are loving and peace-centered. We make most all decisions together. X and I don't fight. We have differences of opinion, but we talk them out and they're done with. Neither of us grew up in homes where people "yelled" at each other. I am eternally grateful for his love and respect for me. I have never once doubted his love, of which I continually thank the Lord. He is a dear, dear man.

As for his relationship with children, they love him! Most of our friends call us second parents to their children. Some dear friends have three boys who think X is the strongest man in the world: the kids love to ride on his feet. He has a wonderful way with children.

I'd love to add a bit about my father. I recently read an article that said "We learn best in an environment that gives us total permission to make mistakes." That is who my father is. As we grew and made mistakes, his gentleness in letting us each see ourselves where we had gone wrong (rather than preach to us about it) has

50

been one of the things that has made me who I am. He is one of the two most loving, generous, caring, wonderful people in the world.

X writing now. I believe L will make a great mom. She has a special ability to communicate with children and make them feel loved and worthwhile. She gives children great personal attention and draws out the best in them. Her spontaneity and energy is a real motivator with children. I believe that our child will have a very good experience with L. I just had to say this!

Thanks for your letter. We are praying for you as your days come close to delivery. We are looking forward to hearing from you soon!

Love,
X and L

January 8, 1990
Dear X and L

It's hard for me to believe you're real people, having to refer to you as X and L! What if I call you Xylophone and Lollipop? If that's ok with you, it sounds more personal. I am so blessed and so loved, but my life has been quite different than yours. You guys sound a lot like my best friend and Lamaze partner. I used to get jealous of her home where nobody fought! But God has shown me that He uses people from all types of backgrounds. I wouldn't trade a thing: my wonderful family, my parents and stepparents, my mistakes, or this child.

I don't believe there has ever been a child more loved than this one. His little life has touched so many friends, acquaintances, family: so many people have come to me with stories. Women who have aborted have shared their grief with me and their joy over my decision, men who have had children aborted, teens who are confused about whether to say "yes" or "no," teachers who have

51

asked me to speak to their classes about adoption, pregnancy, sex, abortion…! It's incredible, the doors that God has opened all because of this one child. And I have gained a respect for myself. For one of the first times in my life, I didn't take the easy way out. All because of Jesus, who loved me enough to discipline me in the form of a child.

I can't tell you how it comforts me to know how much you love this baby. I am not giving him to you because I don't love or want him. Please, please, when the time comes, tell him that. Tell him how much I would've loved to be his mom, how I would've taught him to love and respect people and God, how I would have always tried to be open and honest with him. Tell him that I gave him over to you because you are a family. You are ready for him. God chose you for this. I was chosen to carry him and love him for nine months, after that, he was sent to you.

They say babies can hear inside their mothers, so I talk to him and we listen to a lot of music. Since I was a small child, I have responded to music. I can't tell you what this means. You know that bible verse that says the Spirit prays for us in groans that words cannot express? That is music, for me.

You told me about your father. He sounds wonderful. I am so glad our child will hear loving words from a father. My dad wasn't in our home, and I would never wish that on any child. My mom gave piano lessons after school to make ends meet while we were growing up. Looking back, I can't imagine how she did it! She sacrificed so much for us. It took me a long time to forgive my dad and realize that there are two sides to every coin.

I loved what you said about room for mistakes. I wouldn't be who I am today if it wasn't for the mistakes of myself and others; but most importantly, if it weren't for the love of a God who transforms mistakes. I want you to know: I am not the Christian I should be. I never have been. I have days of doubt, fear, and anger. "There are two of me: one does the right thing, one cannot see." Amy Grant sang that.

Well, the way things look, you will have our child within a month. I think he will be born any day. I have already started dilating and I've been experiencing false labor. I'm not looking forward to saying goodbye, but I am looking forward to starting my life. I finished up my B.A. in English and I have job hunting to do. We'll see where God leads me. Beth knows I want the hearing to be quick. She's doing all she can to speed up the legal process. I don't think I'll feel secure until this baby is with you and out of the shuffle. I want him to bond with you as soon as possible. I hope and pray that his being taken from me and then taken from foster parents won't affect him. I have been sewing for him; I made him a baby quilt and a sleeper to match my nightgown.

I fully agree with any course you take in telling him about me. I don't want to do anything that would confuse or hurt him. But if there is any way I could contribute or watch him grow through you, I would be forever grateful. One of my biggest fears is that he would be lost to me the minute I left the hospital. Judging from you letter, that is unlikely. I am so thankful for your love and openness.

Why did I choose you? I looked over many summaries, and there was always something I didn't like. I liked everything about you. Actually, I patterned my requests after a family that is very dear to me. They are strong, rooted, fun-loving, uncompromising, yet entirely human and not at all "religious." The husband of this family treats me the way he treats his own daughter. I feel such a part of their family. His wife has been incredibly supportive, sending gifts and cards out of the blue. He is adventurous and outgoing. She is practical and generous and gentle. And they have such a fun sense of humor. I love the comfort and joy of this family. You sound a lot like them. It sounds like you would raise our boy like I would, if I could.

I would love to keep writing and writing, but I'll close with what I know of the birth father.

We met at a frat party. He is a basketball player and a business major. He has a beautiful singing voice. It's hard not to be furious at his attitude, and he's had a few run-ins with my hotheaded sisters. Now, we talk. He's trying to be more open and honest with me. His family just doesn't want to talk about it. I believe he cares, he's just one of those people who doesn't know how to show it. We are friends, and I'll be glad to tell our baby that someday. I've tried to encourage him to write you; maybe he will.

I look forward to hearing from you again. You're in my thoughts and prayers.
Love,
Your birth mom

I can't tell you how much these letters settled my mind and heart. They helped to confirm that I was doing the right thing for my baby. Xylophone and Lollipop's (Don and Kiki's) openness, their love for me, their lack of fear and paranoia freed me up to be glad my baby was going to them. Often I have seen adoptive parents who are scared of their children's birth mothers, and I've heard horror stories of birth mothers who have come back after months or years, wanting their babies back. They remind me of the story of when King Solomon, was faced with the two women who were fighting over the same child. Solomon suggested that they saw the child in two and give half to each woman. The first woman agreed, but the second passionately requested that the child be given to the first woman rather than be cut in two. Solomon gave the baby to the second woman. Her love for the child, regardless of her own grief, proved that she was his mother. She was willing to suffer pain and loss to ensure the safety of her child. (1 Kings 3:16-28) Xylophone and Lollipop were willing to risk trusting me. They wanted to get to know me and "our" baby, even if I turned out to be like the mother in Solomon's story that wanted to cut the child in two. If I gave him to them and then later wanted him back, I may as well ask that he be cut in two, such would be the ripping of his heart, not to mention theirs.

Fast forward: Kiki and I were walking across the frozen Ten Mile Lake, watching our children running ahead of us. It was our first weekend together as a family. They had come to Bemidji Friday night for our worship meeting, and then we all packed a bag and went to the cabin, which was, ironically, an hour away, all these years. As we watched the kids running together, Ian shortening his long strides to match Eli's small ones, and our three girls chatting and walking with Karli, Ian's little sister, I kept saying to Kiki that it felt "surreal."

Kiki turned to me and said emphatically, "Take the 'sur' off woman! It's REAL!!"

So much for "I may never see this child again, and I may never have another." Another hope answered.

I love it that Don said, all those years ago, that I sounded like Kiki. The more I get to know her, the more I see he was right. She is a lot like me; just ahead of me. She didn't have all the emotional catch-up and healing to do that I did. Every time I get together with her, I find a little more of myself that I didn't know was there. One goofy example is color. I used to be, years ago, a "white wall" kind of girl. Then I turned into a green girl: everything was green. I still love green. But after visiting Kiki for the first time in her home, which at the time was vibrant shades of red, blue, yellow, green, and orange, I realized that color is who I am. We were remodeling at the time, and my home now resembles the bluffs of Winona in autumn: one of the most beautiful places in the world. (Seriously, Google that) We were at a conference recently where we were practicing hearing God. We had to ask Him about the person we partnered up with- small things like what their favorite color was, and then see if we heard right. The lady who got me said, "You don't have a favorite color. You are full of color." Hilarious.

Another thing Kiki said to me, in the letters so long ago, was that "it takes courage to face the issue" in regards to handling my pregnancy responsibly. What is funny about that now is that I have been told that I am someone of great courage- willing to "plow through anything that comes my way." This was true twenty three years ago as well, but I just didn't know it or see it. Kiki pulled it out. She was doing, automatically, what we try to do every day: pull the "gold" out of people. Find the things about them that are amazing and bring them to their attention.

She still calls Ian "our" boy. Who I was, and who I am becoming, are so much a part of who Ian is becoming. It's a crazy thing, DNA. Both Don and Kiki were willing to be sensitive to the fact that he was adopted, and try to fill in as much for him as they could. They let me be part of their lives for all those years through letters, and now I can show up at their front door.

Ian and I were standing in my kitchen once last year, talking. He was sharing with me how he didn't feel a need to contact his birth father, because Don is his father. I understand that, but then why contact me? He just wanted to. In fact, if there was anyone he was not happy with in our whole scenario, it was his birth father.

It took me a bit for this to sink in. Twenty-three years later, I am standing in the kitchen with my boy, and he is defending me? Telling me that he is not happy with the way his birthfather treated me, treated us? Holding him to a higher standard? I still can't wrap my head around it. It felt like a crazy kind of protection or value that I didn't get from the father, but twenty three years later, I got from the son. My own son, now grown, defending his Mom. A little bit of justice that I didn't even ask for. I didn't even *think* to ask for half the rewards I have seen.

chapter nine

"900 years of time and space, and I've never met anyone who wasn't important"

The Doctor, *Doctor Who*

January 13, 1990

My baby was due today. My friend and Lamaze partner, Mary, said, "Just think. Within the next two weeks, something very major will happen in your life." It's hard to believe. People ask timidly, "Are you scared?" Yeah, I am. Only of the unknown. At this point, I'm more apprehensive about delivery than I am about saying goodbye. Something warns me that it should be the other way around. I love the parents I chose. My child will have a wonderful life, and I won't ever lose him.

January 17, 1990

When you read this, you won't be a baby anymore so I can't call you "my baby." Especially when you aren't only mine. From the very beginning you were "ours." God's, mine, and your parents as you know them. I never saw you as mine alone.

We have been through so much, you and I. It amazes me to think that at this very moment you live inside of me. I have loved you from the beginning. I have regretted what I did, but I have never regretted you.

The choice to give you up was the toughest thing I have ever done. I wished, so many times, that things had been different. But they're not. I need to look at them as they are right now. Today. I do not know what lies ahead for me, so I can't make a decision based on what might be.

I can't wait to meet you. I never expect to be "mom" to you. I chose another woman to be that, and I am eternally grateful to her and her husband for being who they are. If it wasn't for them, I don't know if I could have given you up. I wasn't about to give you to just anyone. As it is, I really feel like I'm giving you to two of my best friends to raise. Through them, I hope to watch you grow.

Even though I will always see you as my child, I will never try to take the place of your parents. I know how much you must love them, and that makes me happy.

I plan to keep in contact with your parents so they'll know what's going on with me over the years. They'll be able to fill in whatever you need to know. And I'll be here, too. Here, hopefully, with your stepfather and brothers and sisters. Even if we never meet, that's okay. You can know that you've always been in me. I will do my best to move on and just let you grow. I have learned much from carrying you.

You are invaluable to me. Have a wonderful life, baby.

How did I know that "I won't ever lose him?" Isn't it crazy amazing how God answered all my hopes, all my dreams for him, for us?

After he was born, I went through a period of confusion. I thought about keeping him and what that would realistically mean. Where would I live? What would I do? How would I pay the bills? Eventually, I went back to my decision for adoption, but it felt good to honestly look at parenting. I knew I had left no stone unturned, and it confirmed my decision to let him go.

It was a sweet and painful good-bye letter to write. It was only a few hours after finishing it that I went into labor.

chapter ten

All this pain
I wonder if I'll ever find my way
I wonder if my life could really change at all
All this earth
Could all that is lost ever be found
Could a garden come up from this ground at all

You make beautiful things
You make beautiful things out of the dust
You make beautiful things
You make beautiful things out of us

All around
Hope is springing up from this old ground
Out of chaos life is being found in You

You make beautiful things
You make beautiful things out of the dust
You make beautiful things
You make beautiful things out of us

Gungor, "Beautiful Things"

The contractions started at ten minutes to midnight on January 17. I had just gotten off the phone with my dad, complaining that I felt sure I'd always be pregnant and I would never have this baby. As I lay down to sleep, I had to run to the bathroom. False alarm. I lay down again, and again I needed to get up and run to the bathroom. After this happened four or five times, I called Mary.

"I think it's time. I feel weird."

"Do you want me to come over?" she asked, sleepily.

"Please!"

She was there within ten minutes, and we talked for a while. Then we decided to get some more sleep, but I couldn't. Finally, at 4:20 am, I called Nancy at Naniboujou Lodge. She had six children, and had helped me a lot with pregnancy stuff when I worked there that summer. She told me to relax, breathe, and call an OB nurse. When I did, they wanted me to come in.

This was it. I think by this time, I was so ready to have him and be out of the awkward, bulky stage, that I didn't think much about it. They admitted me to a welcoming and warm birthing room. Mary promptly fell asleep in a chair.

The contractions were getting stronger, but I could still talk over them. At 7:00, I called my sister Chris. My dad came after that and stayed for the next nineteen hours. He is a teacher and he missed two days of school to be with me. My mom, my sister Kelly, my step dad Bob, many of my friends -all these came and stayed through the actual birth. The room was packed. The hospital had rules about this sort of thing, but I think the doctor and nurses bent them.

When I got really uncomfortable, I requested a painkiller. All that did was numb my brain so I wasn't as aware of what was going on. But I concentrated through each contraction: I was determined to stay in control and not panic. I was grateful for the training Lamaze classes had given me. By mid-afternoon I requested an epidural, which is a painkiller injected into the spine.

I hadn't wanted a spinal block, but it was dragging on so long. My strength was waning. My cervix was only dilated to five centimeters and it needed to be at ten, so we called the anesthesiologist. He tapped my spine, and the rest was a breeze. Within a half an hour I was sitting up in bed, talking and even laughing with friends and family. The nurses would comment, "Does this woman know she's in labor?" Yes, but I was grateful I couldn't feel it!

This continued until midnight. The nurses took such good care of me, and I got some rest. Flowers were already pouring in and I hadn't even had him yet.

Finally, I was dilated. My doctor almost had to use forceps, but with one final boost, Samuel was born. I had been able to faintly feel the contractions over the epidural, and with the aid of the monitor we could see when I was supposed to be helping my body push him out. It's funny how you lose your modesty at times like this. The profundity of what was happening put self-consciousness far away.

All of a sudden, he was there. Samuel Carson: a big 9 pound, 2 ounce, 22-inch long boy. The wait was over. The physical pain was gone.

Just about everyone was in tears. He was whisked off to the nurses' station because he had come out with a little infection due to the long labor. Exhaustion took me. I wanted to hold him, but I hadn't slept in two days.

Within half an hour, everyone was gone. There were lots of kisses and hugs and tears, and everyone went home to bed. It was 2:00 in the morning on January 19, 1990. I fell into the deepest sleep I think I have ever had.

We stayed in the hospital for five days. The nurses were wonderful. Whenever I needed to talk, they were there. They grieved with me. His birth and adoption became an OB floor event. We were waited on continually. Sam and his little crib were rolled into my room, and I mothered him there for that time.

We had so many visitors. Friends brought flowers and cards. My pastor came and dedicated him. Classmates called. I had so many gifts: the room was vibrant in contrast to the barren January outside my window.

I cried a lot during that time. As soon as I would remember that our time was short, I would melt again. People tried to comfort me, but their words fell to the floor. I knew that the decision had been made, and it wouldn't be long before Beth and the foster mother would be there to take him to another home.

At last the day did come. I had spent so many hours watching him, holding him, feeding him, rocking him. I wanted to remember everything about him. How he smelled, how he moved, how he looked. He would look at me so intently: almost like he wanted to remember me, too. I dressed him that day, and I signed the papers to release him to foster care and to New Life.

As his foster mom carried him out, he cried. I cried. The pain of finding out I was pregnant did not compare with the pain of coming to love-and then release- someone I first thought I didn't want when I found I was pregnant with him. I just didn't get it that I would love him so much. The fact that he was sent as a gift by my Father to help me understand that life wasn't casual and that the actions of people affect other people deeply, only added to his worth. He was so beautiful. He smelled beautiful. That something so profound and God-like could be housed in the body of a small child overwhelmed me. I felt like such a wretch that I even considered taking the life of this magnificent person who would grow in the love of two people who longed for him. Who was I to tamper, even consider tampering, with his days, his time on this earth? The sorrow and grief flooded in. I clung to Pam and sobbed. And yet, hidden under the grief, I knew that I was following the road meant for us...the road that was best. It was the only thing that could have held me to it. All the months of planning and praying and releasing had brought me to this, prepared me for this. I knew so intently that this was God's best for him, and for me. I knew it. Somehow that deep knowledge held me that day.

Even now, I look at the whole thing with a sort of awe.

Phil and I have had four more children and one miscarriage, since Ian. So we have five more kids. For any of you reading this who are thinking that every child you have will be a twenty-six hour labor, don't worry. After Ian, my longest labor was about six hours and eventually I moved out of the hospital scene and had Eli at home with a midwife. He was a water birth, a water baby. It was great.

Each pregnancy was different, but at the same time, much the same. The one thing we did notice, was that when I was pregnant with girls, I felt and acted like I had PMS for nine months. When I had boys, I was a rock: steady emotionally. My husband said it was almost uncanny. The biggest thing I would say to you is: give yourself a break. Pregnancy is a big deal for your body, and you are "normal." And after the baby is born, all the hormones are adjusting again to not being pregnant, and you feel "pms'sie" again. Don't trust your feelings at that point, just rest and know they will pass.

I know it sounds crazy, but I experienced this grief again when I met him after twenty years. I still don't really know why. I really think that sometimes your spirit knows stuff that your body and your mind don't, and you cry, and you laugh and you don't know why. It's ok. Give yourself a break in this, too.

You'll read about it; it's in my journals. I analyze it, like I do. In the end, they're all good theories, but I think the reason we grieve is because we love. We really love, and when we see how much our actions affect people around us, we feel that. My giving Ian a life outside of me caused my girls to grieve. Once they were teenagers, they felt his loss, they wanted him in our lives. That doesn't change that I did the best thing for him, for us, back then. But we just grieve stuff, all the same. And it's ok, and it's healthy. It's when we don't grieve that we get stuck.

So just remember that God will never take you where He can't uphold you. If you need to cry, cry. If you need to laugh, laugh. Don't judge yourself, and don't be scared. Your Daddy's got you.

chapter eleven

Never has the weight of one been so heavy
and never has the love of a mother been so strong.
This mother shall lift this child into another life,
and she shall cry heavy tears.

in a letter from my friend, Dan Sundseth

Now began the three-week wait until our court date when I would
terminate my rights to my son. It was a difficult three weeks because I
was compelled to look at all my options again, and I felt like we were in
limbo. He was in foster care, and I wanted him with his parents. Today,
he would have been. The laws have changed. They would have been at
his birth, and he would have left the hospital with them. I still would
have grieved, but knowing he was with Don and Kiki would have, I
think, made things easier.

January 23, 1990

**I don't think anyone can truly understand how it feels to be
sitting here without my son. I'm empty physically, emotionally. I've
never hurt like this in my life.**

**Every time I used to eat, he'd eat, too. Every time I'd sneeze,
he'd jump. I'd rub his back when he'd press up against me, I'd
guide his little foot back when he'd kick too hard in one spot. I'll
never forget his little face.**

**Jesus promises that all things will work together for those who
love God. He promises to give me grace for whatever comes my way.**

64

I still have the option to keep him; sometimes I feel like I'm walking around in hopeless darkness without him. I can't imagine life without him and I can't imagine life with him. With me, he would know love, but also daycare and sometimes a busy, frustrated mother. With his adoptive parents, he would know a mom who could be with him all day. He would know a full-time, loving father and lack of want. And he would also know how much I loved him, me and my family. He would know that he has another name and another family waiting to welcome him back someday.

I miss my baby and the way he looks at me with those big, inquisitive green brown eyes. I kept telling him, "It's okay. Mommy's right here. I'm not going anywhere." He seemed to smile at that.

Love is waiting patiently to see the unfolding of God's plan. Love is trusting that God will guide me. Love is maintaining the hope that God will show me the desires of my heart. Love never fails. Love never ends.

Samuel, I lift my eyes to the hills: where does my help come from? My help comes from the Lord, the Maker of Heaven and Earth. I miss your darling smile. Our bond is so strong: I know that God will keep my love for you in your heart. He will not lead me where His grace cannot hold me. You will be fine. You will know love, joy, and contentment. He will not let your foot slip; He who watches over you will not slumber. I can offer you all that I have, but I wanted you to have more. You will have all your parents can give you; and, in time, you can have me, too.

The Lord is the shade at your right hand. The sun will not harm you by day nor the moon by night. The Lord will keep you from all harm. It was so difficult to put you into His arms instead of mine. (Personalization of Psalm 121)

The days went by sorrowfully, slowly, painfully. My journals ranged from quoting Scripture to swearing in frustration. I was still living with my parents, waiting the three weeks for the court date, reviewing my options. I needed to lay it all out on the table again and again: what would it mean to parent? What were the pros and cons of adoption? I always came back to the same conclusion: adoption. Sam was in foster care for those three weeks in a town forty-five minutes away. I could visit him anytime I liked. I could call Beth and say "I want him" and they would have him to me within twenty-four hours.

I visited him three times in that three-week period. Each time I waited a little longer between visits. We would meet with friends, shop, do whatever you do in a day. Mothering him for those short times was wonderful: I would feed him, rock him, bathe him. He was beautiful. I am thankful I had that time with him.

January 24, 1990

One week ago I went into labor. I miss Sam so much it's all I can do to keep functioning.

God knows what's best. I can't give up my son! But I want the best for him! I've prayed that if God wants me to continue with this, He'll have to give me the will and the grace to do it. Hurt isn't a strong enough word to say how I'm feeling.
Anguish.
Agony.
Torment.
These come closer.
This really sucks.

January 26, 1990
Dear Lollipop

I'm not trying to exclude Xylophone, but I need to write this mother to mother. I want you to know how I feel. I want Sam to someday know what I went through... I want him to understand how I love him. I don't know what to do. I have never in my life experienced such grief.

66

Today is his one week birthday. I have never loved anyone like this. Everything that was so important to me before doesn't mean a thing now. All I want to do is be his mother. It's hard for me to believe that anyone else could want or love him more than me.

I made him pajamas and he wore them in the hospital, but now I sleep with them. His pictures are everywhere. I take pills to dry up my milk and my abdomen is all stretched out and flabby with stretch marks. I'm still bleeding and healing, and he is not here. My family is acting like nothing has happened and I'm in a nightmare.

I have prayed constantly, telling God that I want His best, but if that means giving up Sam, He'll have to give me the will because I can't do it. I fell like my instincts are being ripped out of me.

I need your prayers. I want to do the right thing. I can't imagine life without him, and I can't imagine life with him. He seems to need me. When I hold him he's so content and peaceful. He turns my direction when he hears my voice. He sleeps on my heartbeat and always needs to hold my fingers or examine my face. He knows me. I want him to be safe and loved and happy. I want to give him everything. But I don't want to put him in daycare. This isn't fair.

If Sam goes to you, I'll feel like he's gone to two of my best friends. But I wanted you to understand me, so you could love him more than you do now. So you could tell him how much I love him.

Your birth mom

That was a tough letter to write. After Don and Kiki had been turned down three times, I hardly wanted to turn them down again. But I needed to write that out and I needed to know what it would feel like to say, "I'm keeping him." It didn't feel right. Beth wisely waited until the court date was over and Sam was literally in their hands before she gave this letter to them. I am grateful for that today.

Re-reading these journals is so fun. I'm reading about one of the hardest things in my life, and yet, it's so full of life and hope and joy, that any pain that may have been there is just- gone.

And I love how I said, "this isn't fair." It's so whiney. I love it that I can look back on me and love me. Like the campus pastor that I am, I want to hug me back then and say, "It's going to be ok. If you could only see your future, the weight of this would simply vanish."

It makes me chuckle at myself now, and think of the Grandfather in *The Princess Bride*. "Who said life is fair? Nobody said that." The bottom line is that it wasn't an issue of fairness. Sy Rogers, a great international speaker on the subject of sexuality, said "God forgives. Biology doesn't."

That's about what I was experiencing.

And God, as so eloquently stated in The Shack, says "It's not my purpose to punish it; it's my joy to cure it." He could see twenty-three years into my future, and knew the laughter that would be there. He probably *was* hugging me and saying "It's going to be ok. You have no idea."

chapter twelve

I hear you have a soft spot
For fools and little children
And I'm glad
'cause I've been both of those
I shook my fist up toward the sky
And at most of those who loved me
A frightened angry boy, in grown up clothes
But a Father's eye can always see right through
And a Father's heart can tell when tears are true
Now I'm standing on this road
Your hand has brought me to
Your faithful love will lead me
Farther on

Russ Taff, *Farther On*

February 2, 1990

Deuteronomy 1:31 says, "There you will see how the Lord your God carried you, as a father carries his son..." As a father carries his son.

Your (biological) father carried you once, baby. He came to New Life last week. He walked in with a big teddy bear. I was holding you and you were screaming because your bottle wasn't ready. What a first impression! You settled down when I started to feed you, but when I handed you to him, you calmed completely. It was like you knew who he was.

I think he was overwhelmed. We sat together, the three of us, for about an hour. It felt weird. I felt like I was pretending, like you weren't ours.

We took some pictures of the three of us. I have so much for you, Sam. A whole box full of stuff: cards, letters, rose petals, your birth certificate, our wrist bands from the hospital, loads of pictures; I kept everything. I love you more than myself, Sam. It hurts to give you up. To trust that God will lead me farther on.

Your daddy that you grow (your adoptive daddy) with will carry you a lot, baby. He will give you more than a teddy bear. He will bandage your scraped knees and kiss away your tears. He, and she, your mommy, will do all this for you and for me.

As for me, I will cry for you and pray for you and miss you. But I will have the joy of knowing that I was the one who got to give birth to you after carrying you. I get to give your parents the joy of raising you. This is the one thing, besides knowing that Jesus is taking care of me, that is getting me through our court date. On the day I let you go forever, your life with them will start.

You won't miss me, you won't hurt. God will heal me, in time. Knowing I've helped to create a family and knowing I'll meet that family face to face someday is getting me through. Sweet dreams, baby. Mommy loves you.

Thinking of things associated with motherhood brought tears instead of joy. I would never kiss his little face, watch him grow or play, or teach him about life and faith. My heart was broken. Ruth Stull said, "Pieces will feed a multitude, while a single loaf will satisfy only a little lad."

Maybe my pieces would feed a multitude.

I re-read Xylophone and Lollipop's letters. I talked with Pam and Beth and Mary. I had lunch with my dad, wading through my options. I knew, again and again, that I had come to the right decision for the right reasons. What I knew took over what I felt. I had trained myself in truth for nine months, and it prevailed in the end.

February 5, 1990

"for the Lord your God is gracious and compassionate. He will not turn his face from you if you return to him."

I'm trying. I pray for God to hold me all the time. I said goodbye to my son for the last time today. It was my last foster care visit. I can't tell you how it feels. Of course he cried all the way out, and I kept wanting to run after him and hold him and kiss him again. I tried to notice every touch, every smell, every expression of his today. I don't ever want to forget.

February 8, 1990
Remember always: (to myself)

You are giving your son to the Lord, who will place him in love and safety. He would not have let you go on believing that adoption was the right thing if it wasn't. He would have told you. He loves Sam more than you do. He loves you more than you love Sam.

He has brought you through every panic attack so far. He will bring you farther. All the dark things you imagine are not from God. This is all for a reason : you had the joy of carrying Sam and giving birth to him. But it was God who gave him to you in the first place. Give him back. Don't hold so tight. Let him go.

Lord, help me to trust you.

Writing helped me deal with the grief. I went through so many stages: anger, denial, pity, wanting to fix it or change it, and just sadness. But in the end, because I had thought and prayed and talked so much about it, I accepted it. I embraced the pain. It felt good to know that I had traversed every path, sought out every option. Writing my feelings down -my hurt and anger and frustration -trying to think of the exact

71

words that described how I felt, was a healing process of its own. I can't fathom trying to keep those torrents inside, to let them stew and bubble. Getting things out into the light, writing them down, sharing them, brought enormous clarity.

I embraced the grief in other ways, too. Taking pictures, visiting him in foster care, sleeping with his little pajamas that smelled of his fresh baby smell: I took in all I could before I let him go.

One thing I would do differently if I could would be to read more on the grieving process. If I had, I would have seen that my feelings were normal, and that I would probably be grieving for quite a while. That's just good to know.

What would I say to those women facing a time like this? I would say, stop. Take time to breathe and walk and not hurry. Go away if you need to: find a place like the North Shore. Surround yourself with people who love you and will encourage you in the faith and hold you accountable. Read. Begin a journal. Get yourself into a good church, a good Bible study. Ask God to show you how much He loves you; ask Him to help you to see it, ask Him to open your eyes. We are His beloved, His glorious ones. His plan for our lives is exciting and more filled with life than we can imagine. There are those who walk with God consistently, and they're not usually the ones getting attention on the news. Find them in print, podcast, video... find them in flesh. Be mentored by them, meaning, read what they've written. Learn from them, hang out with them, watch how they live. Let them teach you how to walk with God.

The song "Farther On" was one I listened to constantly during the days after his birth. The comfort it contained was so tangible I listened to it quite literally over and over. The beginning is quoted for you at the front of this chapter. Here is the end:

Life sure has its choices
You've left those choices to me
and I'm glad, but sometimes I feel caught.
It's hard to know which bridge to cross
and which bridge I should be burning
I long to learn, I'm so slow to be taught

But a Father's eye can always see right through
and a Father's heart can tell when tears are true
Now I'm standing on this road
Your hand has brought me to
Your faithful love will lead me farther on.

His faithful love will lead you farther than you thought possible.

A year and a half after I gave Don and Kiki to Ian, I married Phil. We met on that trip to the North Shore that I took with Meg and Mary that I describe in this book. I went home, finished school, had Ian, went through the adoption process, and grieved....all the while with Phil in the back-burner of my mind.

For some reason, he just stuck there.

When I moved to the Shore, I worked at the Lodge again, but also for friends that owned a sled-dog equipment and gear company. I sewed packs upstairs, Phil built dogsleds downstairs.

I could tell you the big, long, slightly-sordid tale of our relationship at the beginning, but can I just sum-up? We were both ...

So

Young.

And I don't mean age-wise. I mean, emotionally. We didn't know how to be a son or a daughter, we just tried to manage the white-water rafting of relationships on our own. We didn't know how to ask for help, and we didn't trust anyone enough to believe they would give it when we asked.

I laugh at it now. We are both amazed at how God was able to take two messy, hurting, grieving, selfish, bull-headed, opinionated people and twenty one years later, you have.....us.

I guess I should have taken my own advice and journaled all that, too. But that would require another book.

My husband is known to say that "any two people can make a marriage work if they keep their hearts humble." I know it's true. If one of us had decided at any point in our marriage to harden our hearts to the needs and feelings of the other, it would be over. Sure we've had times where we've hurt each other, absolutely. We've made mistakes. We've had extended times of misunderstanding. We used to fight, meaning, we communicated to convince the other to see things our way.

Communication can get loud when we're trying to do that. We still have some "intense fellowship" sometimes, but not nearly what it used to be. We've learned to communicate to understand each other, not to win. It's ok to not agree on everything.

And Phil has always taken the lead in this. I'm not proud of this, but if anyone has been the one to hold onto resentment, it's been me. He is almost always the first to apologize and start repairing what needs repairing.

There are some who have wondered: How did Phil feel about all of this? I never thought to ask. So I asked him. He basically said that he didn't think much about it at the time. He remembers thinking that I was brave, and giving Ian a family like I did showed that I had good character. He shared my joys of getting pictures and letters for twenty years, so he knew Ian had a good family, and wouldn't really need him as a father-figure once we all met. So he has simply been a friend to Ian, and enjoyed watching our reunion and helping me process through it, with all the surprising emotions it brought. He has enjoyed watching Ian interact with our girls and Eli. He's happy for us all.

Ladies, find a man like this. Our girls joke about how hard it will be to find a man, after having a dad like theirs. I agree, but I'm confident they're out there.

So we were pregnant with Grace when we married. I used to be really ashamed of this. But I'm not anymore. Yes, we made a mistake. We did. And we made it right, with God and man and each other. And He left us a blessing, and her name is Grace, and I can't imagine life without her. She is love lavished on us, in the midst of our chaos.

In fact, as a campus pastor who attends more weddings than I can count, this is what I tell our newlyweds, or even our "been married for five years now" couples. Having children is opening up yourself to see a face of God that you will never see otherwise. It's the one thing you never regret.

Ever.

We have a bunch of resources to share if you would like to build your communication, relationship, marriage and parenting skills. People probably told me that marriage and life took work, but I never really understood it until the last ten years or so. I have to work to keep growing and learning; I can't just coast. So we train ourselves. We buy

74

and borrow resources. And they are worth every penny, every minute, every effort.

chapter thirteen

Frodo: I can't do this, Sam.
Sam: I know. It's all wrong. By rights we shouldn't even be here. But we are. It's like in the great stories, Mr. Frodo. The ones that really mattered. Full of darkness and danger, they were. And sometimes you didn't want to know the end. Because how could the end be happy? How could the world go back to the way it was when so much bad had happened? But in the end, it's only a passing thing, this shadow. Even darkness must pass. A new day will come. And when the sun shines it will shine out the clearer. Those were the stories that stayed with you. That meant something, even if you were too small to understand why. But I think, Mr. Frodo, I do understand. I know now. Folk in those stories had lots of chances of turning back, only they didn't. They kept going. Because they were holding on to something.
Frodo: What are we holding onto, Sam?
Sam: That there's some good in this world, Mr. Frodo... and it's worth fighting for.

J.R.R.Tolkein, *The Two Towers*. From the screenplay, written by Peter Jackson, Fran Walsh, and Philippa Boyens

February 12, 1990, was the day of our court hearing. Part of it is recorded in my journals.

It seems like a dream, but today I gave you a family, baby. I gave you back to God for His keeping. Your parents saw you for the first time today. I wish I could have been there! I would love to have seen their joy. I know how they must have felt, holding you for the first time. It gives me strength to think about it.

Tomorrow they will take you home. They must have shopped their hearts out today. I can imagine the excitement of setting up a nursery: teddy bears and the smell of baby wipes. They're probably getting ready for you now. I can't imagine they'll sleep tonight.

So tomorrow you'll bring life to that empty nursery. The quilts I made you and the sleeper of yours that I have slept with these three weeks will only be a few of the things gracing that room. I bet it's beautiful.

I feel both a peace and a pain. I love the word bittersweet. It describes so many things. I'm glad I don't have to make any more decisions. I will miss you so much, and I hate that. But you and I have brought life to a family, and I think that's worth it. As long as you're safe and happy and loved, I can deal with the hurt. I know it will fade in time, and I know this is God's best plan. Last night I laid a fleece before God. I asked Him to cause something to happen today that wouldn't have allowed the hearing to take place. A blizzard, a flat tire, whatever. But in fact, we got there without any problems, waded our way through the city, found parking, and everything was on schedule. We even got the judge we prayed for. Everything went as scheduled.

At the hearing, I sat with Beth and Pam. When the judged called on me, I had to stand and tell her why I was relinquishing my son. She wanted to know my reasons. I told her that he needed a mother and a father, and that right now in my life, I couldn't give him that. We prayed that we would get this judge; some other judges, we were told, didn't understand why a woman would first choose to give her baby life and then give him a family. This makes absolutely no sense to me. Why not give him a family?

After leaving the courthouse, I felt a peace that couldn't have come from me. I had just relinquished all rights to my child forever, and I felt remarkably calm. I knew his parents would get a call saying he was theirs, and I knew I didn't have any more decisions to make. I slept hard during the two hour ride home.

February 14, 1990

I guess they were overwhelmed. Beth told me today that they hardly knew what to do with themselves. I'll bet they still can't believe that you're theirs, Sam. They probably think it's all a dream. Sometimes I do.

Beth also said that the first thing your mom said was, "Oh! You hugged her today, didn't you? Let me hug you, it's the closest I can be to her!" She passed the hug on to me and sent the message that they loved me. Your mom is a beautiful woman, Sam. I don't know if I could do better.

Dear Xylophone and Lollipop,

I can hardly describe to you the peace I feel in my heart, knowing Sam is with you. My mind is tired of making decisions. It's a sweet relief knowing God is in control.

Beth told me as many details as she could remember and that I could think to ask. I cried again. Thanks for the hug.

How is he? Isn't he beautiful? I just can't ask enough what you're thinking. I am so blessed to have carried him. He's such a gift. Don't you think?

Hold him for me. Kiss his face and tummy and toes and hands, and tell him he's fabulous and that I love him. I am so happy, but I still miss him!

Love,
Your birth mom

The dedication service was held at the New Life office the day after my court hearing. Everyone was there: Xylophone and Lollipop's parents, siblings, nieces and nephews; and they videotaped the whole thing. I'll see it someday.

Dear Xylophone and Lollipop,

How is it being parents? Day to day, caring for him, experiencing him, how is it? Does he smile yet? Isn't he just perfect?

I had my first job interview today. It went really well. I felt confident. I have this peace I carry with me: I think, "I have a beautiful son. I gave him all I had." And I'm so happy he's with you. Have I said that a lot? I am just so overwhelmed with this joy I feel. I was listening to some tapes on spiritual warfare and they reinforced the fact that we are in a battle constantly. The enemy knows us, wears us down, and waits for opportune times to attack. That is what happened to me. Little by little I compromised until one night, I could have ruined my life, or at least created and destroyed another. But God took over. I look back and can almost see the angels surrounding us, Sam and I, all the way through this.

I'm moving Saturday. I'll be working at the Lodge. The owners, Tim and Nancy, are like family. I'm looking forward to the peace and solitude. I know I have a road ahead yet; I know that this just isn't over and forgotten. I feel like I'm going home.

Thanks. I love you guys.

Once again, I gazed out the window overlooking the lake. The scene was different this time: snow covered the frozen earth, the birches were bare, the spruces dressed in their winter green. The shore of the lake was solid and snow and ice covered it for miles. Only the day before I had hiked in the woods and watched a pack of coyotes finishing off a deer out on the ice. This was the really quiet time on the Shore; I could almost hear the northern lights. My friend and co-worker, Kevin, could imitate a coyote, and we would hear multitudes of them answer as we stood listening in the sub-zero air.

It was hard to believe that almost a year had passed. My Sam was safe and happy with parents who loved him and loved me. Because of my choices, I had given life to a child and to a family. I was, and will be, eternally grateful to God for the strength He gave me.

I felt a deeper peace than I had ever known. Something told me it was an introduction of things to come. Psalm 18: 28-29 says

You, O Lord, keep my lamp burning;
my God turns my darkness into light.
With your help I can advance against a troop,
with my God I can scale a wall.

How could I ever doubt His love again?

Fast forward with me again, twenty- three years: I know this wasn't funny at the time, but it is now. After the court hearing, Anne and Beth (the social workers) went out for lunch. They realized half-way through their lunch that they had forgotten to call Don and Kiki and tell them that all was well! Can you imagine? They were probably wondering….all sorts of crazy things! We chuckle at it today, but wow. I bet that was scary for them then!

I still haven't seen the dedication service. Reading this manuscript again has reminded me; I'll ask Kiki next time I see her. She's got it in a file somewhere! Maybe when we go for the MN reception.

It's interesting, reading about the peace I had after the court hearing. That happens anytime I make a big decision, even today. There is some anxiety about it, but once I've made it and do it, there is peace when it was the right thing to do. Giving Sam/Ian a family was one of the best decisions I have ever made, and since that day I have felt peace whenever he would come to mind.

chapter fourteen

"I want to be a healer, and love all things that grow and are not
barren."

J.R.R Tolkein, *The Lord of the Rings*

Phil and I have three girls and one little man: Grace, Ilsa, Maddie,
and Elijah. Grace is quirky, creative, and sees life from an angle that I
have never even considered. She's an artist and a writer, and has
embraced anything steam punk. She has a novel in the works. She loves
people wherever she goes, and she's even learning to have mercy on the
ones that aren't so easy to love.

Ilsa, our center child, was the one baby who did not want to see the
world. She wanted to snuggle. No front-facing baby carriers with this
one; she wanted to bury herself inside your jacket, as close to your
heartbeat as possible. She is a seer, a dreamer, an artist, and a musician.
People cry when they hear her sing. In a good way.

Maddie is our princess. I don't just mean she likes clothes and shoes,
of which she does. I mean, she knows who she is. She knows she's
royalty, and she lives like that. She organized her Easter candy by color,
type, and size when she was little. She climbed trees in her dresses and
heels. She helps her friends in high school do the heart-work of forgiving
those who have hurt them and embracing their God-identity. Even just
last night, she was helping a friend forgive his mom as they were texting.

Eli wants to be the next Tony Stark (genius robotic creator of comic
book fame) when he grows up. This kid has a grasp of computers and
technology that I cannot even comprehend. His brain is wired to be doing
something that takes his full attention, and still hear the conversations
going on around him. When his "heart hurts," he comes to us and we
help him deal with it. He loves math, science, video games and potty

humor, and can't understand why in the world cursive writing was ever invented, much less forced upon third-graders.

We told the girls about Ian when they were probably eight, six, and four. We didn't want him to be a big surprise, and yet we wanted to wait until we thought they could understand. Come to think of it, we probably told Grace much younger, I just can't remember exactly. They seemed to do well with the knowledge. Grace missed him most of all. She even had a dream that she called him at one point. He knew who she was, in the dream, and he said to her, "I need to talk to you later. Is that ok? Later." The tone was happy, not sad. I think the oldest child just always wants an older sibling, and she wanted him. She didn't have to wait too long.

For myself, I thought of him over the years. The pain got less intense as the months and years went by, and as I received letters and pictures from Don and Kiki. Their love for me and their willingness to be part of our lives brought peace to the whole situation. Phil was my rock through all the emotions: he always seemed to know that one day, we would reunite.

I did have my times, as you've read, where my longing to know him was more intense. I didn't really let myself hang on it too long.

Phil and I had a family we were close to on the North Shore, Joel and Kathy. We're still close today. Their kids were little when Phil and I were dating, and now they're all grown, and two of their three are married with kids of their own. We spend Thanksgiving with them every year. One year, Joel's nephew was killed in a plane crash; it was a terrible tragedy. He was in his early twenties. Not long after his death, Joel and Kathy's daughter Josie, along with a bunch of people, ran Grandma's Marathon in Duluth to commemorate their cousin's death and remember his life. Joel and Kathy, along with many friends and family of the young cousin, attended.

Afterwards, they had a gathering. Josie told me later that she and her parents were sitting with Joel's sister, the mother of the young man who died, and some of their closest friends. These friends were asking Joel and Kathy where they were from, and when they told them "the North Shore" (All Minnesotans know that means "the north shore of Lake Superior") - and mentioned Naniboujou Lodge, they said, "Oh! The birth-mother of our son lived and worked up there during her pregnancy!"

Realization dawned on our friends…the friends who grieved Ian's loss with me, friends who were there with us as we started our little family together. Josie said that her dad took the woman's hands, kissed them, and said "You have our Sam." She said she had never seen her dad so emotional.

Joel and Kathy's nephew died in a plane crash. This boy who died, his parents, are Don and Kiki's good friends. It seems that we were "placed" in the same family. I gave Ian to Don and Kiki, and as he grew, he knew Joel and Kathy's family, as they were Don and Kiki's dear friends. He probably played with the boy who later died tragically in the plane crash. And Phil and I call Joel and Kathy our family; I met them just after placing Ian. So all those years, we had no idea that were one connection away from each other.

They spent the weekend sharing stories. I got a call from Joel & Kathy afterward, detailing the whole event. It was so encouraging at the time, because we didn't know Ian yet, and we didn't know when we would. Or if we would.

It was just so good that I still can't quite get my heart around it.

And so we lived our lives and raised our kids and got healthier emotionally and spiritually and physically as time went on. We moved from the kind of people who felt afraid and the need to control our surroundings, to the kind of people who trust God and each other and live in freedom, managing ourselves. On a good day. I think it's a journey we're all on, whether we know it or not.

So, the day came, as I always knew it would, and I never thought it would. It was a bright and cold January morning, twenty years after I had given birth to Sam. Twenty years earlier I had held him and cried in a hospital room, facing the greatest loss of my life. Here is the journal entry from that day:

January 19, 2010

I have a headache from crying and laughing. God is so good, so good, so good.

Most of you know that 20 years ago today, I had a son. Twenty years ago right now I was holding him in a hospital room. I was not

married, not even in a relationship. His father was a decent guy, but not ready to parent. Even if I had been mature and selfless and ready to parent myself, I wanted this baby to have a mom and a dad, both. I had no guarantee of a husband who would be willing to love my baby. So I found him a family and gave *them* to *him*. That sucked. It wrenched my heart out. I grieved for a year or more. I didn't know I would love him so much.

I thought it would be easy, maybe.

But the little bit I knew about God, I knew my son would be safe, and loved. I somehow did it, gave him that family, and moved on with my life.

Since then, I've married, had three gorgeous daughters and one little fabulous man. My husband rocks. God has brought us through so much weather- good and bad- and brought us to Bemidji to minister to college students here at Bemidji State University. So not only do we have four children, we have dozens of kids. American, African, Nepali, Korean. We love them all.

But I have this son, somewhere. I wrote his story and had it published. *The Gift of Sam.* His story is amazing. His mom has kept in touch with me all these years, sending me letters, pictures, stories. Many times she has said to him, "Honey, your story is amazing." And he has said, "Yep, Mom, I'm good."

Until ten days ago. Ten days before his 20th birthday, she said again, "Honey, your story is amazing." And for the first time, he said, "Really?"

So over the next several hours she and his dad tell him: about me, about his birth, about my husband and our kids and what we do now, about the book ("There's a BOOK?" "Yes! Everyone has read it!" He sees the cover and says, "Is that me?") about our God-sent mutual friends....everything. They brought out all our newsletters and pictures and showed him... he has three sisters (in addition to his little sister with his family) and one brother! Glorious day! She waits to tell me until the time is right. Then this morning, on the 20th birthday, she calls me to tell me that my son, our son, wants us.

The nightmares are silenced. He doesn't hate me. He loves me; he loves his siblings. Oh Jesus, you are more than I can speak!

Two hours later, I have given up on mascara for the day. Understatement. My son has read the book written about him, the book that has travelled the world and encouraged young women to see their babies as gifts, not problems to be fixed. Women in Korea, Australia, China, America- I have heard their stories. Children are alive today because of my son.

His mother, Kiki, relayed everything I said to him an hour ago on the phone. (She was taking notes!) Apparently his roommate has read the book too and has told him to "just call her!" She asks him, "Is there anything you would like to say to her?" When the silence on the phone indicated to her that he was hesitant to speak with his roommate in hearing, she added, "Like, you would like to meet her too?" He said, "Yes, I would agree with that!"

We meet every Friday night at our home to worship. We sing, pray for each other, pray for our city and our schools and our country and the sick. We are determined to do what Jesus did and more, just like He said. When Kiki told me that he was possibly willing to meet us, I told her about Fridays and invited their whole family up. She said to him, "Well, your dad has next weekend off, and the Thoofts have invited us up for the weekend." He said, "Mom, that would be great."

Do you hear me? Do I hear me? My son is coming next weekend!!?!?!??

Do you suppose I will ever stop crying today? Laughing? I think I need some Advil. Then coffee. Then call my sisters.....

85

That was a really, really joyful day. Walk with me through the next year:

January 21, 2010

I posted a note on my Facebook about the recent call I received from my son's mom with the news that he wants to meet us. I can't describe the noise my heart made that day. My husband got a little of it on the phone. My kids heard it. But I can't describe it.

So two days later, a dozen phone calls later, thirty odd comments later, and one call from a friend who works at a newspaper: I have come to a few things.

Suddenly, MY story is not just mine anymore! Wow. That alone sort of shakes my world. Second, I can't anticipate anything. People ask me what do I think of this or that or how are we going to do that or are we sure we want to do that or....and I think: I can't think. I actually had to put it out of my mind yesterday and paint my bedroom.

This is crazy. I have a son and I don't know him at all. I am about to embark on a life long journey to get to know him. I don't really have any fears. Maybe a few small ones lurking behind doors waiting to jump out and bite my legs, but nothing roaring in my face.

I think about the person I was when I gave birth to him. I remember the day I let the foster care mom take him away from me. I still feel it. I lived for the next meeting. It was difficult to let anyone else hold him. The nurses commented on the obvious bond between us.

I looked at every option from every angle. Reality would be: me working full time and him in daycare. I had no offers of help from family, except my sister. Something told me she and I couldn't handle it. Reality would be up nights, no sleep, work, pay the daycare. He would grow up and I would see half of it.

So my thinking was this. For me: I wanted him. I didn't' want to give him up. I could work, I could love him and take care of him. Reality for him: being raised 40 plus hours a week by someone else, a mother who loves him, no father.

I know many people don't have fathers. Many turn out beautiful. But I so wanted one myself...I wanted to hear the words from my dad....you're beautiful, you're fun, you're smart, you couldn't do anything to make me love you more nor anything to make me love you less. I wanted that time with him, books read on the lap, Frisbee in the yard, so many scenarios. I could keep him, but I could not guarantee him a dad, the one thing I wanted so badly.

So, with the help of my Heaven-Dad, I found him one. A couple: a Mom and a Dad. He had a good job; she could stay home and raise him. They could play Frisbee in the yard, go camping, read books. She could get up at night with him without stress. They had 15 or so years of maturity over me, had gone through all the stuff and came out strong, solid, sure. They were un-offendable, non-judgmental, full of concern and love for me as well as him. And I'm not painting a picture; I know these things to be true.

I am close to the day when I have to look him in the face: that face that looks like a man-version of me, and tell him why I let him go. Making my coffee this morning I thought of it. Oh God what am I going to say?

Fast forward fourteen years from his birth. I am married to Phil; we have three amazing daughters. Seriously, they knock me over every day with their beauty, their hearts. Then we have a son; Eli was born six years ago. I was kind of....clueless about having a son. We just didn't have a toolbox for boys. We knew girls. Girls are easy, sort of. They teach you to walk tenderly. They crush easily. They shine and the glow sticks to you all day long. But a boy? How do we do boys?

When we had him, it took a negative five seconds to adore him and understand that we were in for a new journey full of rocking fun. This kid gets me every day. Climbs on my lap and kisses my face and tells me how beautiful I am, how he wants to marry me when he grows up but Daddy got there first, how I'm the best Mommy in the world. Then he jumps off and starts killing bad guys with his Legos or dinosaurs or whatever.

And I realized, when Eli was born, what I had missed, with Sam. And the ache grew deeper and started all over.

So last week I was in Target and thought of him, again. I have thought of him over the years, but not so much as the last few years. Maybe because of Eli, maybe because we share our lives with young adults and Ian is their age now. Every time I see a John or a James or a Mark, I see my son. I am at our SALT conference and expect to walk right into him. I scan crowds. So I was in Target and thought of him and the ache returned, and I said, "Jesus, if it's going to be awhile....years....can you please just take him out of my heart? I can't do this, this aching for him. I have to live life and love my kids..."

And then a week later I get the call. I feel like I am upside down, but its ok. I will tell him all these things, or he will read them, maybe.

I had to tell Eli. We have never told Eli; he's only six. He has heard us talk about Sam, he has seen pictures, but I don't know what goes through a six year old boy's mind. I don't think he's lost sleep over it.

I found him in his room, putting together some sort of bomb with Legos. I got on my knees, so I could be face to face. I told him I had something I wanted to tell him. How can a six year old boy understand that his Mommy gave up a son once, and won't do the same to him? Why did you give him up and keep me? Are you going to give me up too? Oh, God the wrenching-

So I just told him. I told him that once I married his Daddy, I would never ever give any of my children to anyone else. I only wanted Sam to have a Daddy and a Mommy. (Can he get this? Or am I making it worse? But I have to tell him. He's going to meet him next week? Oh help!) I finish stumbling over words that are dropping out onto the floor...

He blinks the kind of blink that swallows stuff. He looks at me and says, "I understand, Mom." Then, "I have a brother?"
"Yes, honey, you do."
"And he wants to meet ME?"

chapter fifteen

And I am convinced that nothing can ever separate us from God's love. Neither death nor life, neither angels nor demons, neither our fears for today nor our worries about tomorrow—not even the powers of hell can separate us from God's love.

Romans 8:38, New Living Translation

More journals from our first year. More processing:

March 16, 2010

I've been thinking of how I'm going to answer him. Why did I give him up? I knew the biggest issue for me was the father thing. But all I could ever tell you was that I wanted one and somehow knew it was important. I could never get past just the daily stuff, the love languages: quality time, affirming words, acceptance, all that.

It feels like deep calling to deep.

This is what I heard this morning: When we lose the concept of family we lose the reality of the Kingdom. The absolute cry of the human heart is for a genuine father. When we have that, we know who we are, why we are, who we belong to.

Then we perform because we are part of that family, not to earn a part in that family. We do what we do because of love and acceptance and family, not to earn a place in love and acceptance and family.

So I gave Sam a family: not just so his dad would play Frisbee in the yard or his mom would stay home with him. He needed a full picture of God; he needed to know who he is, whose family he is a part of. He needed to know those things so he would grow up sure.

And he has. Kiki has told me dozens of times: "He's just so happy with who he is." A kid in his graduating class said, "Every guy in our class wants to be like Ian." It wasn't just about me or my family that is connected by blood to him. That's partially it. God has brought him to a place where he wants to know that connection. It's more than that.

He's bringing the big picture together.

All creation groans waiting for the sons of God to be revealed. All creation GROANS waiting for US to figure out *who we belong to, who we are, why we are....*

So if we've experienced abuse or neglect in an earthly father, our identity becomes distorted. We forget who we are. This Father thing is a big deal. Somehow I knew, twenty years ago, that a father was really, *really* important. I should have known there was a bigger picture, of course!

So my prayer for me, for my children and my husband and all our students, and my prayer for my son and his family, and you whoever is reading this: is that we would begin to experience the Father's love deeper in our spirits than we ever had before. That we would encounter Him. That we would KNOW who we are and why we are and to whom we belong. It seems to me, that would solve so much.

March 22, 2010

Friday night, after twenty years, I met the son I gave up. We had knots in our guts, so did they. They called when they got to Bemidji. When they pulled into the driveway, I could hardly believe it was happening. Out of the red Jeep Cherokee steps a man, not a boy. The girls ran out to meet him. He opened his arms and hugged them all, and looked up at me and waved. Bare feet kept me at the door. Ok, so maybe more than bare feet. I had to catch my breath and pick my heart up from the floor.

I wish I could describe that feeling: him hugging his sisters, calling them by name. Then walking toward me. I still hadn't caught my breath when he put his arms around me and whispered "thank you" in my ear. Twenty years ago I let foster parents carry him away from me, and here I was watching him walk back. All I could think to say was "I love you." We were right in the doorway, and it was cold, or I wouldn't have let go so soon.

His mom and dad and sister filed in; we were all talking at once. I grabbed his little sister Karli and hugged her.

So many things to describe. All night I kept looking his way. I just wanted to gaze at this boy, the "Man Cub" as his mama calls him. It fits, and he likes it, so I've adopted it as well. His face. The eyes are mine; the smile is mine. The square feet are mine. His mom was so amazed at our feet!

Once during worship, I caught his gaze and held up my hands as if I was taking a photo. He did the same.

Nightmares silenced indeed. My son loves me.

After Friday night worship, and our world meeting them, we pack a bag and head to their cabin near Walker. I think we got to bed at 2 am. Phil and I were up before everyone else, finding a spot to ponder, coffee in hand, overlooking the frozen lake.

He lets me talk, lets me hug him more times than I can remember or count. I say, "Ian, this is so weird." He says, "I know. It's awesome."

Stories, stories all weekend. Kiki kept saying, "thank you, thank you...." and I kept saying, "No, thank you, thank you..." She wondered how she could thank me. "Sharing him with me, with us, was more than I could ever imagine," I told her. She just keeps acknowledging that it's all from God. She has no fear of me; she is not threatened by us. I am overwhelmingly loved, and I can't get my head around it.

When Ian sees us together, he calls us "the mamas." I am his little brown mama and she is his tall blonde mama.

Eventually we were able to sit at the kitchen table, the three of us, Kiki, Ian and I. He has heard our story from his mom, and he read the book, but he let me tell it. It felt so good to tell it myself, right to his face. The thought that he would feel abandoned was the one fear that would wake me up at night. When I told him that, he shook his head. "No. Never." And his answer to how he felt when he thought of the adoption? "I just thought, 'I don't know enough about that,'" so he would dismiss it. What kind of metal is this man made of? He didn't judge what he didn't know? Is that possible? I just talked to my friend Pam recently, Pam who was with me during my pregnancy with Sam/Ian, Pam who was there the day the foster parents took him from the hospital, Pam who has been my friend these 20 years...and she reminded me that we prayed before he was born and we prayed when the foster parents took him away and we prayed after I signed the papers, and we've prayed all these years-that he would never feel abandoned, that he would always know he was loved.

Prayers are being answered as I write.

I don't want to put the man on a pedestal. Kiki actually sent him out of the room once because she didn't want to puff him up, we were glowing about him that much. He is extraordinary, just not on a pedestal. I have learned so much from him already. God has used him as a picture of His love for me. I can't get it; I need to get it. I have no grid for this. Jesus, build me one.

I gave him this family because I wanted him to have a father. God gave them because he wanted to give him an identity, a fortitude.

I looked up fortitude: it means a mental and emotional strength in facing difficulty, adversity, danger, or temptation. He acts like the prince that he is, but would never think to call himself that. He loves without agenda. The sense of humor is fabulous. His confidence is securely anchored in humility. I have met people like this before, but not many. I am so blessed to know him, I am so proud of who he is, who he has become. To think I had a little part in that gives me joy. To think I will see him again; I can't get my head around it.

So we had this amazing weekend: we played cards, he taught us to play Settlers, and we had meals and drank oceans of coffee and looked through pictures and watched clips of high school musicals and listened to John Meyer, and I will tell more as the days go by, but Sunday afternoon did come eventually, as I knew it would. I was praying all Saturday, "God, help me deal with tomorrow, when we have to leave again." Why why why? He's back. Why is it so hard to leave?

I think, as I told his mom after he drove away, it felt too much like the moment they took him away twenty years ago, that wrenching separation. I know this is different, I do. It is. But the feeling was still there and it was too familiar. The wondering, "Will I ever see him again?"

Same kind of different.

I think I was just surviving the tidal wave.

Once again, I got the grace I needed. He drove away last night, having hugged us all, waving and yelling, "Bye family!" This morning I woke up at home, and the tears came again. What?! My husband spends a lot of time counseling with men who are getting free of addictions, and he is always helping them name how they feel. It's so important, because when you can't name how you're feeling; you tend to go do things to try to rid yourself of this stuff you can't name.

So... grief. This feels so much like grief. C.S. Lewis pointed out once that grief feels like fear. It does. But it's not. It's not. I think, I know, this grief I'm feeling is natural, probably good. I held him and loved him and kissed him as a baby, and now, all those things I was able to do, restrained, of course! He's not a baby, or a little boy anymore. Twenty years. I missed twenty years. Like I took a nap and woke up and boom, what happened?

I have a beautiful life, have had a beautiful life in those twenty years. I would not trade an ounce of it. I told him I would do it all again for him, I would.

The something missing- the missing his babyhood, his childhood, the closeness of mother and son, missing that. That is what I am grieving. And, on top of that, as my amazing husband points out, "Well, you're happy! And you miss him!" Of course. So wrap all that up in one mind, one hormonal female body, and voila! Another day of wasted mascara.

So can I just say again: I don't regret it, any of it. He had such a happy childhood, such a loving family, that I would never change it, even if I could. He wouldn't be the man he is had I raised him. I told his mother early on that I would never be a "nightmare birth-mom."

And I meant it. I still don't want to be that. Somehow I have to work out what that means. I have many hopes, and God holds those. I will say I have become an instant Sioux fan, and Rugby is one of my favorite sports.... (Ian goes to UND and plays rugby)

And it all comes down to this, this thought I keep having in the midst of this roller-coaster emotional ride I am on. My God gave him to me when I least deserved him, my God gave him a family who exceeded my hopes and expectations in their love for him and me and mine. My God brought him back to me twenty years later. How could I doubt what my God will do now? I can't imagine, but I also cannot doubt. I have seen too much, I know too much! This grief I feel, is just that: a feeling. Feelings pass and give way to truth if we let them. The truth is, He has added to our family this year. And, I am thinking, it has only just begun.

I got to thinking about this fact that it took twenty years to see this prayer realized. God was working it all, working many angles of it, for twenty years. I heard snippets, through letters, but I didn't get the full picture of my answered prayers for twenty years.

I know there are Biblical characters, and stories since then, of the same thing. Promises taking twenty, or more, years to come to pass. But when they do, dang. Look out. The tidal wave will rock your life.

So I've been thinking. Can I rest and be patient and believe that He is working on all my hopes? All of my prayers? Can I be patient and know He hasn't forgotten? Even if it takes twenty years?

I mean, seriously. How long did Abraham wait for a son? Sixty years?

It seems to me, if I know my Father, my Daddy - if I know His heart towards me - I can be patient. It seems to me it all boils down to intimacy with Him. So no matter what mess I find myself in, or what mess you find yourself in, just hang on to that. Know Him, really know Him. I'm not talking about religious notions of Him or rules or laws. I'm not even talking about *just* the Bible. The early church didn't have the Bible as we know it today. They had the Holy Spirit; they had *Him.* I think we need both. If we don't have both, I think we get kind of slanted in our view.

Anyway, my own story is teaching me to have faith. Even still. Every time I read it.

April 17, 2010

Well, good news. I haven't cried since Monday. Until tonight.

What's the deal? I am not a "crier" by nature. I figure this grieving thing is gonna take some deep wells until it's dried up, I'm ok with that. But I guess I thought I had it pretty well finished. I mean, how much is in there, seriously? I know there are storehouses of snow and hail, but tears?

Today we took Grace and our friend Abbie to the Fargo airport. They are on their way to northern California: Abbie for a week, Grace for two weeks, until we get there, as we're meeting her out there for a conference. It's a big long amazing story how it all came about and I won't go into that here. So as I was mapping our trip, it occurred to me that Grand Forks, where Ian is going to school, is fairly close....quick check with Map Quest and it's 40 miles further to go see him. He's up for it, so we do a loop.

Eli is wound up, from I don't know what for sure; somebody was slipping him sugar, I think. The girls are the girls, chattering and laughing and enjoying this new big brother experience. Phil and I mostly watch and listen and enjoy them all. We eat dinner, see the dorm room, meet some friends, carry on about how neither of us can keep our eyes open for a picture...

Then it's time to leave. He's a college student. He's got skates to sharpen and French to study and a hockey game to play. We have two hours to drive. Hugs all around, and he directs us out of town.

And then, the floodgates. What?!? Why? I just saw him! Why am I crying again? I'm starting to feel like a drama-queen-thirteen year old, for Pete's sake.

So I think, and cry. I told Kiki today that I might as well be Joel's daughter; I think like he does. I think about something, and then I think it through again and then look at it from another angle and then check it out upside down and sideways and then make sure it doesn't shock me backwards. Why am I crying? I know it's the grieving thing; I missed his childhood. Ok, so get over it already. He's right here. He's found you. He's invited you into his life. Be happy. I am happy, but I cry a lot.

Then I got to thinking about how he's so content with his life. He doesn't need me, he's got a mom and dad. It kind of makes me sad that he doesn't need me, but then after thinking it through, (upside down and sideways!), it makes me happy. He doesn't need us; he wants us. That's cool.

And then I was thinking how it hurts to drive away from him. I choked to Phil, "is it going to be like this every time?" He said probably. But, he said, it will probably get easier.

Then my brain wandered to how sometimes we just avoid this stuff so we don't have to hurt. I mean, how much easier would my life be if I never met him? No grieving, no tears, no wrenching separation every time he leaves. I mention this to Phil. I am learning to actually talk about the things I am thinking to him, because he's a really good processor, and he sees the bigger picture. He points out a pretty profound thing: no pain, no gain.

Sounds like a Nike commercial, but he's right. How many people do we know who don't bother to walk through the pain to get to anything good? There's a conflict with a friend; someone said that someone else said something that, if true, really hurt and was unjustified. But we don't really know for sure, but we're too afraid of the possible pain to find out, thus the friendship ends. Or church. Someone does something we don't understand, so we leave. Or, to be a little more painful, GOD does something we don't understand or don't have a grid for, so rather than dig into it and find out if our faith is just too small for Him, we blame it on whomever and leave, thus wrapping our unbelief in nice theological words. (I ain't pointing, baby, I've done it.) Whatever the circumstance. No working out equals no strength. No disciplining a child (with LOVE!!), no disciplined child. There may be pain in the night, but joy comes in the morning.

Is anyone willing to work through the pain to reach a deep friendship? I am as guilty as anyone. I do have a full handful of heart/soul/take-a-bullet-for-you-and-vice-versa-friends that I have gone through difficulties with that are now dearer for the crises we've been through. And they are the friends I can call in the middle of the night.

So my bottom line?

Ian is worth every tear, every wrench of my heart, every "sword that pierces my soul." He is worth knowing, as he is now. It is kind of interesting that he has invited us into his life at a time when he is finding his own feet, so to speak. College is typically a time when young people pull away from their families a bit, think their own thoughts, find their own way.

And he is inviting us in, just because he wants to.

So I text him today, and say this: "I think it may take me awhile to NOT want to tell you every day that I love you. Hope that's 'all good!'"
His response?

"Oh, take your time. Love you too!"

June 9, 2010

Even when I'm not actively thinking about it, it seems my brain is processing. All the time. And I started to realize why I cry every time I leave him. Actually, this last time- we met in Duluth for a night, all of us except Phil and Don who couldn't come - I didn't cry. Weird. Or maybe not so weird.

Can anything really be normal in this scenario?

I am thinking that I cry because when I see him it's sort of like a concentrated twenty years. In the span of whatever time we have. Wow, so crazy, because my spirit is grieving something that my brain can't grasp. I don't know if I can really even describe it. I see him now, as he is, and I can sort of see the little boy there. The little boy with questions and quirky, funny sayings, and sunburned freckles and tired tears. I have another little boy, and I see the giant Lego constructions and the sheer glee on his face and the wonder and the "I just need to snuggle with Mom" moments. I get it all.

With Ian, I missed it all.

So I think that's why I grieve. He comes walking out of his dorm and I catch my breath because he looks, and walks, and gestures, JUST like my dad. It throws me. And I haven't known any of this until now, and I have to take all 20 years in at once, when I see him.

He is so much like me. I enjoy who he has become so much. I am so honored....so honored....that his mom and dad would share him with me, with us.

I just can't quite get over it. I said that to him, when my friend Becky and I met him in Grand Forks and went to hear Paul Young, author of *The Shack*, speak. I said, "Do you think I'll ever get over it?" He answered, "If you're anything like the other mama, no, you won't get over it."

So there you have it. I'm never going to get over this. Suits me just fine.

January 28, 2011

When he was born, it took me about a year to be able to talk about him and not become an emotional puddle.

We are almost at one year now, since our reunion.

100

Ian spent his summer in Alaska. I can almost feel it. It was so *me* when I was his age; it still is in many ways. We live in the north woods. Have stopped to listen to the wolves at the end of our driveway. We tried to get to a rugby game this fall, but there was only one we could see, and it didn't work out. So we'll try again this spring.

But he has come here. A few weeks ago, he came on a Friday afternoon, tuned his guitar, and plugged in with us on Friday night. He led worship with his mama and sisters. It was crazy. Crazy amazing.

I remember thinking that if I tried to think about this, I just wouldn't get it. So I put the thinking aside and just enjoyed our evening. He crashed in Eli's bed and we all had brunch in the morning.

At one point, the girls and I broke into singing various songs from musicals, like we do. Suddenly remembering that Ian has never been with us when we break into family craziness, I look over at him, eating cinnamon rolls at the table, just like he always has. He just fits. His whole family just fits.

And he stays for a while and we load him up with cinnamon rolls to take home and he leaves to get back to studying.

It took a few days for me to remember that I didn't cry.

I know that none of this can really stand in dealing with the death of a loved one. I didn't grieve a death; I grieved a loss and a gain. But it's some sort of point of reference, anyway.

So this summer, the girls and I are competing in a triathlon. I've always wanted to do it; it's sort of on my bucket list. In my hometown, where Ian was born, they have one that is officially "The world's biggest little triathlon." A quarter mile swim (eeeegads!) a ten mile bike, and a 5k. The girls and I have engaged the help of a personal trainer friend, and we start training next week. We have 160 days. I have a long way to go.

But heck, the first thing I knitted when I learned to knit was an alpine sweater with three colors. No scarves here. Why waste time? So why not start with a triathlon?

I have invited Ian to join us. If he's not in Alaska, of course. I have no idea where his summer will take him, but I am sure that if he can be there, he will. I plan to invite his family too, and we will have a reunion. My folks, sisters, families. His family.

You know, last summer our family spent a weekend with Ian's family at the cabin. Ian wasn't there, but we all went anyway! Near the end of our stay, Ian's grandparents arrived. From what I understand, they are a quiet sort. I exchanged an emotional hug with them, like they had things they wanted to say but couldn't find words.

I know I have grieved; I know this has been hard. But when I think of all the people who were given life besides my son, (his parents, their parents, family, friends- the list seriously goes on with long scraggly tendrils), my grief is infinitely small in comparison.

And my grief, to my great joy, seems to be gone.

The weekend I spoke of here was the first year we did the Trinona. It was the weekend I won the canoe. The Trinona has become our yearly reunion weekend. I plan to run that race until I can't anymore. It's more than a race: it's sort of a culmination, and a beginning. We run past the hospital where he was born, swim in the lake that I played in growing up, bike the bluffs that now inspire the colors of our home. It's our roots, all of us.

Ian has naturally grafted into our family. 9 year old Eli and Ian are buddies. Ian grabs him, throws him over his shoulder, and carries him around upside down. Eli falls asleep on Ian's knee, Bionicles in hand.

They haul out their tubs of Legos and build for hours. Ian has just kicked into being a big brother to a little guy, and Eli loves Ian like he was always part of our lives. We found, after meeting, that Don and Kiki call Ian "E" and we call Eli "E." So sometimes, we will shout, "E!" and they will both shout "what?"

Our girls have a great relationship with Ian, too. It was a beginning for them, and it grows every time we see him. We all go about a month without seeing each other, and then notes will start popping up on each other's Facebook: "eye ms ewe." That kind of thing. So we plan to get together, and we do, and then we're all good for a month or so. So far, that's how it rolls. It's like we need fixes.

Just like a parent with any grown child, I suppose. This is my first attempt at relationship with a grown child who lives elsewhere, so I'm learning as I go! You know, you spend time when you can, you let them know when you're thinking of them and what memories or thoughts are bringing you joy, you text or email or call and tell them how amazing they are and how much you love and enjoy them. You pray and declare God's promises over their lives.

And you never stop thanking God that He ever thought, way back in the beginning, to give you a child like this. A relationship like this, a person like this who you can practice loving. You stand in awe of all of it. You see how fabulous and different they all are and you just bubble with joy. And when the day comes that they require your forgiveness, just like normal mortals, you forgive them and thank God for them just the same. As you hope they do for you.

And then you realize that it's all worship. And you're so, so grateful.

chapter sixteen

So Heaven meets Earth like a sloppy wet kiss
and my heart turns violently inside of my chest
I don't have time
to maintain these regrets when I think about
the way
He loves us

John-Mark McMillan, "How He Loves"

It was 5:15 am when the alarm went off. It didn't surprise me because I hadn't slept much anyway. I was too nervous. This was my second triathlon, so you would think the nerves would be calmer, but they just weren't.

Part of it was I was pretty sure I slacked on my training, compared to last year. I worked hard on the swimming, but only had done a handful of bikes and "wogs" – my walk/jog combination. Mostly, Phil and I had been lifting weights and swimming.

So race day was a little scary.

But we hauled ourselves out of bed, strapped on our swimsuits and running shorts, grabbed coffee and bagels and cream cheese (of which we hardly ate any) and Phil drove us to the Trinona race grounds.

Our girls were nervous too. But as a woman in my forties who keenly remembers how automatically in shape I was as a teen, I knew they would be fine, and they were.

As we tagged our bikes and entered the transition station to set up our towels and shoes and water bottles, I heard a voice shout at me and I looked up, "Why are we doing this again?" There was the teasing face of Ian, who had arrived before us and already had his stuff set up. "Why did I let you talk me into this?"

We all laughed. We were all nervous, but we could laugh at ourselves. This is a really good thing.

We set up our areas and made it to the pre-race meeting on time. We did some stretching. We waited for our waves to be called.

Ian went first, then Ilsa and Maddie next, and then my wave of women 35 and over. Once the countdown started, the adrenaline really started pumping, and before I knew what I was doing, I was in the water.

We all nailed the swim, and the bike. Meaning, we shaved minutes of last years' time. Ian did markedly better than he expected he would do. My kids were all ahead of me, and I knew I would be the last one in, but I was determined to not be the LAST one in, like the previous year. I wasn't (yay!). As I rounded the corner for the last tenth of a mile to the finish line, I heard my husband shout, "Run it in, honey! Ya gotta run it in!"

I told you I hadn't trained as much. On top of that, it was 95 degrees with sweltering humidity. I was about done with this grueling race! But then I looked up and Ian and Ilsa were running towards me. "Come on Mama! Let's run it in! You can do it Mama!"

My son and my daughter ran me to the finish chute. I felt two things: one, that my body would collapse at any second, and two, complete joy and disbelief that I was finishing a triathlon with my kids. ALL of my kids.

Would I ever have thought, twenty three years ago as I grieved in that hospital room, that I would be right back here again, finishing the race with this family? I dreamed some pretty big dreams, but not this big.

As we neared the chute, Ian and Ilsa broke off, and I took the finish line alone. I got to run through the tape myself. Several joyful faces approached; one hung a well-earned medal around my neck, one took the timing chip off my ankle, one handed me two bottles: Gatorade and water.

Next time, I am going to be sure to thank those lovely people.

And then, my husband and son were there. Ian grabbed me and engulfed me in a big man-cub hug, telling me how proud he was of me. Then my husband.

Joy, joy, joy.

Boy-Joy. That's what his mom always called him. Well, I got boy-joy and girl-joy going all over the place these days.

Makes me think of an event most assuredly in my future, in your future. In whomever's future that chooses it. I've heard it said that we can look to see what God has in heaven and pull it down to earth, therefore fulfilling Jesus' prayer: "Thy Kingdom come, Thy will be done, on earth as it is in heaven." On *earth as it is in heaven*.

So my friend, you just hang in there. There is nothing in heaven or on earth that can separate you from His love. Everything can be a great adventure. More than you ever, ever thought possible. Dream big, dream wild. You belong to the King of the universe, and His mind, no one can fathom.

And I know that in the end, that will quite literally fix everything.

acknowledgments

I have this overwhelming need to *know* that these people know I love and appreciate them:

Aaron and Jill and your beautiful babies- for sharing wells of encouragement that knows no bounds. And for your help in formatting and editing, thank God!

Chris and Brit- for always loving us

Jaakob- for the humor and insight and generosity and fun you've brought to our family

John & Elizabeth- for sharing your talents so generously, and for always being our kids

Mark Ewert- for being there every single friggin' day

Shawn – for your sharp eyes and kind words!

Cat and Jess- once again, for your love

The Henkelfamily- we love you

Adam- for making us your family, and for being my favorite computer guru

Dave and Becky – for encouraging us to find our hearts again

Our family here: Andy and Megan, Brad and Cheryl, Todd and Sara, Chad and Wendy, Jeremy and Missy, Karl and Melissa, Todd and Karen, Rick and Char, Bill and Becky, our entire Sozo team, Justin and Ruth, Vern and Mary, Niek, Becky, Pastor Jan, Dewayne, Chris Paskevan,

Byron and Mary, the Nelson family, all of you, far and near, and our entire First family and Friday Night Worship family

All of our Chi Alpha students, past and present: we love you all! Our Chi Alpha staff family, all over the world – you are our heroes.

New Life Family Services- for fighting the great fight

Pam and Andrea- my oldest friends, you're the best

Joel and Kathy and family- for welcoming us whenever, even major holidays!

Our entire XA support team: you amaze us, every day

Mom and Bob and Dad and Sue and Kelly & Chris and your families- for still being part of this story, and being the funnest family ever

Don and Kiki, Ian and Chaley and Karli – for being part of our family, and sharing your lives with us

Chuck and Sally and all of our UMD peeps- for letting us be part of your family

Bob and Louise and Elise- my favorite outlaws

Charlie and Cathy and family- for your relentless honor

Mike Amiot- the most honorable, courageous, integrous leader this side of the Rockies. You *are* Chi Alpha.

And Lynne- for taking us in, twice, and pushing me to get this thing finished!

And thank you to Bethel Church in Redding, CA: You don't know us, but God used you to save our lives. We love you.

about the author

Michelle is a cool person who is beautiful and funny and a brilliant writer and everyone loves her.

Aaron Reini, co-author of *Flight of the Angels*
http://www.facebook.com/FlightOfTheAngels

Ok, so this is really funny. Aaron formatted this book for me. He and his wife, Jill, are two of our former students, and great friends. He left a bunch of stuff blank for me to fill in—my own sources, acknowledgements, etc. On this page, he expected me to fill in my own "about the author" so he wrote the above, thinking I would delete it.

I just cannot delete that.

So, I chuckle as I write, but here's my "about the author." I am a wife and a mom and a pastor and a musician and a writer and a triathlete and a gardener. I am a "fly by the seat of my pants" kind of gal, and I am finally starting to see that this is ok. I do what needs to be done. My house isn't always clean, but by the grace of God, my heart is.

contact

Questions for Michelle?
Email me at michelle@dareu2love.com

For more information including speaking engagements and availability, upcoming books, resources, and links, visit www.dareu2love.com.

Facebook: Like us on
https://www.facebook.com/YouSmileWhenYouShowMeGrace

Follow Michellekayt on Twitter at https://twitter.com/michellekayt

One Last Note from the Author: If you have enjoyed *You Smile When You Show Me Grace* and believe it is worth sharing, would you take a few moments to tell your friends about it? I would also be very grateful if you could rate the book and leave a review on Amazon.com. Your words of support will help me get the journal companion, *You Laugh as You Heal Me,* out as quickly as possible.

Thank you!

Michelle Thooft

sources

Prologue

Enger, Leif. *Peace Like a River*. N.p.: Wheeler Pub., 2002. Print.

"Run wild with the hope" Rich Mullins. "Calling Out Your
Name." *Songs*. Reunion Records, 1995. CD.

"Trinona." *Trinona*. N.p., n.d. Web. 04 Apr. 2013.

We-no-nah Canoe. N.p., n.d. Web.

Chapter One

Tolkien, J. R. R. *The Fellowship of the Ring: Being the First Part of The
Lord of the Rings*. Boston: Houghton Mifflin, 1993. Print.

"like Jacob wrestled the angel" "Genesis 32:22-31." *Holy Bible*. N.p.:
Zondervan, n.d. N. pag. Web.

Chapter Two

Young, William P. *The Shack: A Novel*. Newbury Park, CA: Windblown
Media, 2007. Print. Page 7: "one of my main love languages" - 5 Love
Languages

"one of my main love languages" - Chapman, Gary D. *The Five Love
Languages: How to Express Heartfelt Commitment to Your Mate*.
Chicago: Northfield Pub., 1995. Print.

"The Avengers." *IMDb*. IMDb.com, n.d. Web. 14 Mar. 2013.

Lewis, C. S., and Pauline Baynes. *The Lion, the Witch, and the Wardrobe*. New York: HarperCollins, 1994. Print.

"Jesus is perfect theology" Bill Johnson of Bethel Church, www.ibethel.org, said that, but I don't remember where. Probably in a podcast, of which you can listen at www.ibethel.tv.

"The Passion of The Christ - A Mel Gibson Film - Official Movie Website - Icon Productions." *The Passion of The Christ - A Mel Gibson Film - Official Movie Website - Icon Productions*. N.p., n.d. Web. 14 Mar. 2013.

"I only manage me," "manage myself," and "my normal" Danny Silk of Bethel Church, www.lovingonpurpose.com, says those things, many times in many places. His books and DVDs are available on his website. He has taught us how to live, and we are forever grateful.

Chapter Three

Milne, A. A. *Winnie the Pooh*. [Burbank, Calif.]: Mouse Works, 1994. Print.

"About Us." - *New Life Family Services*. N.p., n.d. Web. 14 Mar. 2013.

"The Naniboujou Lodge and Restaurant : HOME." *The Naniboujou Lodge and Restaurant : HOME*. N.p., n.d. Web. 14 Mar. 2013.

"God has two books: the Bible and Nature" I honestly don't remember where I heard that. But my guess is that I heard it on Bethel TV (www.ibethel.tv). You can subscribe for free and listen to sermons and worship sets, or you can purchase a subscription for more access and options.

Montgomery, L. M., and Jody Lee. *Anne of Green Gables*. New York: Grosset & Dunlap, 1983. Print.

Isaiah 41:10, *Isaiah. The Holy Bible,*. New York: Douay Bible House, 1941. Print.

"Bemidji State University." *Bemidji State University*. N.p., n.d. Web. 14 Mar. 2013.

Chapter Four

D.C.Talk, *Mind's Eye. Jesus Freak*. The ForeFront Communications Group, 1995. CD.

Fetal development: "Fetal Development Week by Week | Pregnancy Images | BabyCenter." *BabyCenter*. N.p., n.d. Web. 14 Mar. 2013.

"Lonliness is a lie not to be believed" Again, I heard that on Bethel TV and immediately wrote it on a sticky note and stuck it on our fridge. Whomever said it, thank you.

"fourteen years" I was speaking of Pastor Richard Wurmbrand. You can read his story either on his website, www.persecution.com, or in his book, of which you can request a free copy at http://www.persecution.com/public/tfc.aspx. It is called Tortured for Christ.

"I will never leave you nor forsake you" Hebrews 13:5. *Hebrews. The Holy Bible*,. New York: Douay Bible House, 1941. Print.

Danny Silk: *Loving On Purpose*. Danny Silk, n.d. Web.

"arrested for child abuse!" and "God can win with any hand" Bill Johnson said these, in a sermon. I'm afraid I don't know which one, but he has said it several times in sermons and books. www.ibethel.tv.

Psalm 16:3. *Psalms. The Holy Bible*,. New York: Douay Bible House, 1941. Print.

Paragraph beginning with "Sometimes things like pain and loneliness" I learned these things from Dawna DeSilva (www.bethelsozo.com) She has a DVD and CD called Shifting Atmospheres, and you can purchase it at www.store.ibethel.org.

Tolkien, J. R. R., and Alan Lee. *The Return of the King*. Boston: Houghton Mifflin, 2002. Print.

Chapter Five

Young, William P. *The Shack: A Novel*. Newbury Park, CA: Windblown Media, 2007. Print.

Chapter Six

Calling Out Your Name, Mullins, Rich. *Songs*. Arista Records/Word Records, 1996. CD.

Lewis, C. S., and Pauline Baynes. *The Lion, the Witch, and the Wardrobe*. New York: HarperCollins, 1994. Print.

"Trinona." *Trinona*. N.p., n.d. Web. 14 Mar. 2013.

Chapter Seven

Young, William P. *The Shack: A Novel*. Newbury Park, CA: Windblown Media, 2007. Print.

"take every thought captive" 2 Corinthians 10:5 *Corinthians, The Holy Bible,*. New York: Douay Bible House, 1941. Print.

"The Parent Trap." *IMDb*. IMDb.com, n.d. Web. 14 Mar. 2013.

Chapter Eight

Upton, Jason. *Great River Road*. Gotee Records, 2005. CD.

1 Samuel. The Holy Bible,. New York: Douay Bible House, 1941. Print.

story of Solomon & babies 1 Kings 3:16-28.
1 Kings. The Holy Bible,. New York: Douay Bible House, 1941. Print.

"the gold out of people" Yep, you guessed it. I heard it on Bethel TV and it got transported to a sticky note that was on our fridge for a long time.

Chapter Nine

Doctor Who TV show. *Doctor Who*. N.d. Television.

Chapter Ten

"Gungor "Beautiful Things"" *YouTube*. YouTube, 30 Apr. 2010. Web. 14 Mar. 2013.

Chapter Eleven

"The Princess Bride." *IMDb*. IMDb.com, n.d. Web. 14 Mar. 2013.

I personalized Psalm 121 on these pages. Basically I just wrote it in my journal and adapted it to be talking about me and Ian.

"God forgives. Biology doesn't." Sy Rogers, international author and speaker, wrote that. His website is http://www.syrogers.com/ Any time you get a chance to hear him, do it! The man radiates grace.

Young, William P. *The Shack: A Novel*. Newbury Park, CA: Windblown Media, 2007. Print.

Chapter Twelve

"Farther On - Russ Taff." *YouTube*. YouTube, 27 Sept. 2011. Web. 14 Mar. 2013.

Deuteronomy 1:31. *Deuteronomy. The Holy Bible,*. New York: Douay Bible House, 1941. Print.

"for the Lord your God is gracious and compassionate" 2 Chronicles 30:19. *2 Chronicles. The Holy Bible,*. New York: Douay Bible House, 1941. Print.

Chapter Thirteen

"The Lord of the Rings: The Two Towers." *IMDb*. IMDb.com, n.d. Web. 14 Mar. 2013.

Psalm 18: 28-29.
Psalms. The Holy Bible,. New York: Douay Bible House, 1941. Print.

Chapter Fourteen

Tolkien, J. R. R. *The Lord of the Rings,*. Boston: Houghton Mifflin, 1967. Print.

"Iron Man." Cartoon. N.p.: n.p., n.d. Print.

"Chi Alpha : Minnesota | Reaching University Students." *Chi Alpha Minnesota RSS*. N.p., n.d. Web. 02 Apr. 2013.

Chi Alpha Campus Ministries, USA. N.p., n.d. Web. 02 Apr. 2013.

"Same kind of different." I saw this as a book title once and it has stuck with me. I haven't read the book, but Kiki has, and she loved it! Hall, Ron, Denver Moore, and Lynn Vincent. *Same Kind of Different as Me*. Nashville: Thomas Nelson, 2006. Print.

"MapQuest Maps - Driving Directions - Map." *MapQuest Maps - Driving Directions - Map*. N.p., n.d. Web. 02 Apr. 2013.

Chapter Fifteen

Romans 8:38, New Living Translation. *Romans*. *Holy Bible: New Living Translation*. Wheaton, IL: Tyndale House, 1996. Print.

Lewis, C. S. *A Grief Observed*. San Francisco: Harper & Row, 1989. Print.

Abraham and Sarah, Genesis 17-18. *Genesis*. *The Holy Bible: New International Version*. Colorado Springs, CO: International Bible Society, 1984. Print.

Chapter Sixteen

McMillan, John Mark. *How He Loves*. "John Mark Mcmillan How He Loves." *YouTube*. YouTube, 28 Aug. 2009. Web. 14 Mar. 2013.

"Your kingdom come" Matthew 6:10, *The Holy Bible: New International Version*. Colorado Springs, CO: International Bible Society, 1984. Print.

Made in the USA
Lexington, KY
17 October 2013